FREE Study Skills DVD Offer

Dear Customer,

Thank you for your purchase from Mometrix! We consider it an honor and a privilege that you have purchased our product and we want to ensure your satisfaction.

As a way of showing our appreciation and to help us better serve you, we have developed a Study Skills DVD that we would like to give you for <u>FREE</u>. This DVD covers our *best practices* for getting ready for your exam, from how to use our study materials to how to best prepare for the day of the test.

All that we ask is that you email us with feedback that would describe your experience so far with our product. Good, bad, or indifferent, we want to know what you think!

To get your FREE Study Skills DVD, email <u>freedvd@mometrix.com</u> with *FREE STUDY SKILLS DVD* in the subject line and the following information in the body of the email:

- The name of the product you purchased.
- Your product rating on a scale of 1-5, with 5 being the highest rating.
- Your feedback. It can be long, short, or anything in between. We just want to know your impressions and experience so far with our product. (Good feedback might include how our study material met your needs and ways we might be able to make it even better. You could highlight features that you found helpful or features that you think we should add.)
- Your full name and shipping address where you would like us to send your free DVD.

If you have any questions or concerns, please don't hesitate to contact me directly.

Thanks again!

Sincerely,

Jay Willis
Vice President
<u>jay.willis@mometrix.com</u>
1-800-673-8175

IELTS

General Training and Academic Secrets Study Guide 2020 & 2021

IELTS Book for Academic & General Training

Practice Test Questions

Step-by-Step Exam Review Video Tutorials

Written and edited by the Mometrix College Placement Test Team

Printed in the United States of America

This paper meets the requirements of ANSI/NISO Z39.48-1992 (Permanence of Paper).

Mometrix offers volume discount pricing to institutions. For more information or a price quote, please contact our sales department at sales@mometrix.com or 888-248-1219.

Mometrix Media LLC is not affiliated with or endorsed by any official testing organization. All organizational and test names are trademarks of their respective owners.

Paperback
ISBN 13: 978-1-5167-1224-3
ISBN 10: 1-5167-1224-2

DEAR FUTURE EXAM SUCCESS STORY

First of all, **THANK YOU** for purchasing Mometrix study materials!

Second, congratulations! You are one of the few determined test-takers who are committed to doing whatever it takes to excel on your exam. **You have come to the right place.** We developed these study materials with one goal in mind: to deliver you the information you need in a format that's concise and easy to use.

In addition to optimizing your guide for the content of the test, we've outlined our recommended steps for breaking down the preparation process into small, attainable goals so you can make sure you stay on track.

We've also analyzed the entire test-taking process, identifying the most common pitfalls and showing how you can overcome them and be ready for any curveball the test throws you.

Standardized testing is one of the biggest obstacles on your road to success, which only increases the importance of doing well in the high-pressure, high-stakes environment of test day. Your results on this test could have a significant impact on your future, and this guide provides the information and practical advice to help you achieve your full potential on test day.

Your success is our success

We would love to hear from you! If you would like to share the story of your exam success or if you have any questions or comments in regard to our products, please contact us at **800-673-8175** or **support@mometrix.com**.

Thanks again for your business and we wish you continued success!

Sincerely,
The Mometrix Test Preparation Team

Need more help? Check out our flashcards at:
https://mometrixflashcards.com/IELTS

TABLE OF CONTENTS

Introduction

Thank you for purchasing this resource! You have made the choice to prepare yourself for a test that could have a huge impact on your future, and this guide is designed to help you be fully ready for test day. Obviously, it's important to have a solid understanding of the test material, but you also need to be prepared for the unique environment and stressors of the test, so that you can perform to the best of your abilities.

For this purpose, the first section that appears in this guide is the **Secret Keys**. We've devoted countless hours to meticulously researching what works and what doesn't, and we've boiled down our findings to the five most impactful steps you can take to improve your performance on the test. We start at the beginning with study planning and move through the preparation process, all the way to the testing strategies that will help you get the most out of what you know when you're finally sitting in front of the test.

We recommend that you start preparing for your test as far in advance as possible. However, if you've bought this guide as a last-minute study resource and only have a few days before your test, we recommend that you skip over the first two Secret Keys since they address a long-term study plan.

If you struggle with **test anxiety**, we strongly encourage you to check out our recommendations for how you can overcome it. Test anxiety is a formidable foe, but it can be beaten, and we want to make sure you have the tools you need to defeat it.

1

Secret Key #1 – Plan Big, Study Small

There's a lot riding on your performance. If you want to ace this test, you're going to need to keep your skills sharp and the material fresh in your mind. You need a plan that lets you review everything you need to know while still fitting in your schedule. We'll break this strategy down into three categories.

Information Organization

Start with the information you already have: the official test outline. From this, you can make a complete list of all the concepts you need to cover before the test. Organize these concepts into groups that can be studied together, and create a list of any related vocabulary you need to learn so you can brush up on any difficult terms. You'll want to keep this vocabulary list handy once you actually start studying since you may need to add to it along the way.

Time Management

Once you have your set of study concepts, decide how to spread them out over the time you have left before the test. Break your study plan into small, clear goals so you have a manageable task for each day and know exactly what you're doing. Then just focus on one small step at a time. When you manage your time this way, you don't need to spend hours at a time studying. Studying a small block of content for a short period each day helps you retain information better and avoid stressing over how much you have left to do. You can relax knowing that you have a plan to cover everything in time. In order for this strategy to be effective though, you have to start studying early and stick to your schedule. Avoid the exhaustion and futility that comes from last-minute cramming!

Study Environment

The environment you study in has a big impact on your learning. Studying in a coffee shop, while probably more enjoyable, is not likely to be as fruitful as studying in a quiet room. It's important to keep distractions to a minimum. You're only planning to study for a short block of time, so make the most of it. Don't pause to check your phone or get up to find a snack. It's also important to **avoid multitasking**. Research has consistently shown that multitasking will make your studying dramatically less effective. Your study area should also be comfortable and well-lit so you don't have the distraction of straining your eyes or sitting on an uncomfortable chair.

The time of day you study is also important. You want to be rested and alert. Don't wait until just before bedtime. Study when you'll be most likely to comprehend and remember. Even better, if you know what time of day your test will be, set that time aside for study. That way your brain will be used to working on that subject at that specific time and you'll have a better chance of recalling information.

Finally, it can be helpful to team up with others who are studying for the same test. Your actual studying should be done in as isolated an environment as possible, but the work of organizing the information and setting up the study plan can be divided up. In between study sessions, you can discuss with your teammates the concepts that you're all studying and quiz each other on the details. Just be sure that your teammates are as serious about the test as you are. If you find that your study time is being replaced with social time, you might need to find a new team.

Secret Key #2 – Make Your Studying Count

You're devoting a lot of time and effort to preparing for this test, so you want to be absolutely certain it will pay off. This means doing more than just reading the content and hoping you can remember it on test day. It's important to make every minute of study count. There are two main areas you can focus on to make your studying count:

Retention

It doesn't matter how much time you study if you can't remember the material. You need to make sure you are retaining the concepts. To check your retention of the information you're learning, try recalling it at later times with minimal prompting. Try carrying around flashcards and glance at one or two from time to time or ask a friend who's also studying for the test to quiz you.

To enhance your retention, look for ways to put the information into practice so that you can apply it rather than simply recalling it. If you're using the information in practical ways, it will be much easier to remember. Similarly, it helps to solidify a concept in your mind if you're not only reading it to yourself but also explaining it to someone else. Ask a friend to let you teach them about a concept you're a little shaky on (or speak aloud to an imaginary audience if necessary). As you try to summarize, define, give examples, and answer your friend's questions, you'll understand the concepts better and they will stay with you longer. Finally, step back for a big picture view and ask yourself how each piece of information fits with the whole subject. When you link the different concepts together and see them working together as a whole, it's easier to remember the individual components.

Finally, practice showing your work on any multi-step problems, even if you're just studying. Writing out each step you take to solve a problem will help solidify the process in your mind, and you'll be more likely to remember it during the test.

Modality

Modality simply refers to the means or method by which you study. Choosing a study modality that fits your own individual learning style is crucial. No two people learn best in exactly the same way, so it's important to know your strengths and use them to your advantage.

For example, if you learn best by visualization, focus on visualizing a concept in your mind and draw an image or a diagram. Try color-coding your notes, illustrating them, or creating symbols that will trigger your mind to recall a learned concept. If you learn best by hearing or discussing information, find a study partner who learns the same way or read aloud to yourself. Think about how to put the information in your own words. Imagine that you are giving a lecture on the topic and record yourself so you can listen to it later.

For any learning style, flashcards can be helpful. Organize the information so you can take advantage of spare moments to review. Underline key words or phrases. Use different colors for different categories. Mnemonic devices (such as creating a short list in which every item starts with the same letter) can also help with retention. Find what works best for you and use it to store the information in your mind most effectively and easily.

3

Secret Key #3 – Practice the Right Way

Your success on test day depends not only on how many hours you put into preparing, but also on whether you prepared the right way. It's good to check along the way to see if your studying is paying off. One of the most effective ways to do this is by taking practice tests to evaluate your progress. Practice tests are useful because they show exactly where you need to improve. Every time you take a practice test, pay special attention to these three groups of questions:

- The questions you got wrong
- The questions you had to guess on, even if you guessed right
- The questions you found difficult or slow to work through

This will show you exactly what your weak areas are, and where you need to devote more study time. Ask yourself why each of these questions gave you trouble. Was it because you didn't understand the material? Was it because you didn't remember the vocabulary? Do you need more repetitions on this type of question to build speed and confidence? Dig into those questions and figure out how you can strengthen your weak areas as you go back to review the material.

Additionally, many practice tests have a section explaining the answer choices. It can be tempting to read the explanation and think that you now have a good understanding of the concept. However, an explanation likely only covers part of the question's broader context. Even if the explanation makes sense, **go back and investigate** every concept related to the question until you're positive you have a thorough understanding.

As you go along, keep in mind that the practice test is just that: practice. Memorizing these questions and answers will not be very helpful on the actual test because it is unlikely to have any of the same exact questions. If you only know the right answers to the sample questions, you won't be prepared for the real thing. **Study the concepts** until you understand them fully, and then you'll be able to answer any question that shows up on the test.

It's important to wait on the practice tests until you're ready. If you take a test on your first day of study, you may be overwhelmed by the amount of material covered and how much you need to learn. Work up to it gradually.

On test day, you'll need to be prepared for answering questions, managing your time, and using the test-taking strategies you've learned. It's a lot to balance, like a mental marathon that will have a big impact on your future. Like training for a marathon, you'll need to start slowly and work your way up. When test day arrives, you'll be ready.

Start with the strategies you've read in the first two Secret Keys—plan your course and study in the way that works best for you. If you have time, consider using multiple study resources to get different approaches to the same concepts. It can be helpful to see difficult concepts from more than one angle. Then find a good source for practice tests. Many times, the test website will suggest potential study resources or provide sample tests.

Practice Test Strategy

When you're ready to start taking practice tests, follow this strategy:

UNTIMED AND OPEN-BOOK PRACTICE

Take the first test with no time constraints and with your notes and study guide handy. Take your time and focus on applying the strategies you've learned.

TIMED AND OPEN-BOOK PRACTICE

Take the second practice test open-book as well, but set a timer and practice pacing yourself to finish in time.

TIMED AND CLOSED-BOOK PRACTICE

Take any other practice tests as if it were test day. Set a timer and put away your study materials. Sit at a table or desk in a quiet room, imagine yourself at the testing center, and answer questions as quickly and accurately as possible.

Keep repeating timed and closed-book tests on a regular basis until you run out of practice tests or it's time for the actual test. Your mind will be ready for the schedule and stress of test day, and you'll be able to focus on recalling the material you've learned.

Secret Key #4 – Pace Yourself

Once you're fully prepared for the material on the test, your biggest challenge on test day will be managing your time. Just knowing that the clock is ticking can make you panic even if you have plenty of time left. Work on pacing yourself so you can build confidence against the time constraints of the exam. Pacing is a difficult skill to master, especially in a high-pressure environment, so **practice is vital**.

Set time expectations for your pace based on how much time is available. For example, if a section has 60 questions and the time limit is 30 minutes, you know you have to average 30 seconds or less per question in order to answer them all. Although 30 seconds is the hard limit, set 25 seconds per question as your goal, so you reserve extra time to spend on harder questions. When you budget extra time for the harder questions, you no longer have any reason to stress when those questions take longer to answer.

Don't let this time expectation distract you from working through the test at a calm, steady pace, but keep it in mind so you don't spend too much time on any one question. Recognize that taking extra time on one question you don't understand may keep you from answering two that you do understand later in the test. If your time limit for a question is up and you're still not sure of the answer, mark it and move on, and come back to it later if the time and the test format allow. If the testing format doesn't allow you to return to earlier questions, just make an educated guess; then put it out of your mind and move on.

On the easier questions, be careful not to rush. It may seem wise to hurry through them so you have more time for the challenging ones, but it's not worth missing one if you know the concept and just didn't take the time to read the question fully. Work efficiently but make sure you understand the question and have looked at all of the answer choices, since more than one may seem right at first.

Even if you're paying attention to the time, you may find yourself a little behind at some point. You should speed up to get back on track, but do so wisely. Don't panic; just take a few seconds less on each question until you're caught up. Don't guess without thinking, but do look through the answer choices and eliminate any you know are wrong. If you can get down to two choices, it is often worthwhile to guess from those. Once you've chosen an answer, move on and don't dwell on any that you skipped or had to hurry through. If a question was taking too long, chances are it was one of the harder ones, so you weren't as likely to get it right anyway.

On the other hand, if you find yourself getting ahead of schedule, it may be beneficial to slow down a little. The more quickly you work, the more likely you are to make a careless mistake that will affect your score. You've budgeted time for each question, so don't be afraid to spend that time. Practice an efficient but careful pace to get the most out of the time you have.

6

Secret Key #5 – Have a Plan for Guessing

When you're taking the test, you may find yourself stuck on a question. Some of the answer choices seem better than others, but you don't see the one answer choice that is obviously correct. What do you do?

The scenario described above is very common, yet most test takers have not effectively prepared for it. Developing and practicing a plan for guessing may be one of the single most effective uses of your time as you get ready for the exam.

In developing your plan for guessing, there are three questions to address:

- When should you start the guessing process?
- How should you narrow down the choices?
- Which answer should you choose?

When to Start the Guessing Process

Unless your plan for guessing is to select C every time (which, despite its merits, is not what we recommend), you need to leave yourself enough time to apply your answer elimination strategies. Since you have a limited amount of time for each question, that means that if you're going to give yourself the best shot at guessing correctly, you have to decide quickly whether or not you will guess.

Of course, the best-case scenario is that you don't have to guess at all, so first, see if you can answer the question based on your knowledge of the subject and basic reasoning skills. Focus on the key words in the question and try to jog your memory of related topics. Give yourself a chance to bring the knowledge to mind, but once you realize that you don't have (or you can't access) the knowledge you need to answer the question, it's time to start the guessing process.

It's almost always better to start the guessing process too early than too late. It only takes a few seconds to remember something and answer the question from knowledge. Carefully eliminating wrong answer choices takes longer. Plus, going through the process of eliminating answer choices can actually help jog your memory.

Summary: Start the guessing process as soon as you decide that you can't answer the question based on your knowledge.

7

How to Narrow Down the Choices

The next chapter in this book (**Test-Taking Strategies**) includes a wide range of strategies for how to approach questions and how to look for answer choices to eliminate. You will definitely want to read those carefully, practice them, and figure out which ones work best for you. Here though, we're going to address a mindset rather than a particular strategy.

Your chances of guessing an answer correctly depend on how many options you are choosing from.

How many choices you have	How likely you are to guess correctly
5	20%
4	25%
3	33%
2	50%
1	100%

You can see from this chart just how valuable it is to be able to eliminate incorrect answers and make an educated guess, but there are two things that many test takers do that cause them to miss out on the benefits of guessing:

- Accidentally eliminating the correct answer
- Selecting an answer based on an impression

We'll look at the first one here, and the second one in the next section.

To avoid accidentally eliminating the correct answer, we recommend a thought exercise called **the $5 challenge**. In this challenge, you only eliminate an answer choice from contention if you are willing to bet $5 on it being wrong. Why $5? Five dollars is a small but not insignificant amount of money. It's an amount you could afford to lose but wouldn't want to throw away. And while losing $5 once might not hurt too much, doing it twenty times will set you back $100. In the same way, each small decision you make—eliminating a choice here, guessing on a question there—won't by itself impact your score very much, but when you put them all together, they can make a big difference. By holding each answer choice elimination decision to a higher standard, you can reduce the risk of accidentally eliminating the correct answer.

The $5 challenge can also be applied in a positive sense: If you are willing to bet $5 that an answer choice *is* correct, go ahead and mark it as correct.

Summary: Only eliminate an answer choice if you are willing to bet $5 that it is wrong.

Which Answer to Choose

You're taking the test. You've run into a hard question and decided you'll have to guess. You've eliminated all the answer choices you're willing to bet $5 on. Now you have to pick an answer. Why do we even need to talk about this? Why can't you just pick whichever one you feel like when the time comes?

The answer to these questions is that if you don't come into the test with a plan, you'll rely on your impression to select an answer choice, and if you do that, you risk falling into a trap. The test writers know that everyone who takes their test will be guessing on some of the questions, so they intentionally write wrong answer choices to seem plausible. You still have to pick an answer though, and if the wrong answer choices are designed to look right, how can you ever be sure that you're not falling for their trap? The best solution we've found to this dilemma is to take the decision out of your hands entirely. Here is the process we recommend:

Once you've eliminated any choices that you are confident (willing to bet $5) are wrong, select the first remaining choice as your answer.

Whether you choose to select the first remaining choice, the second, or the last, the important thing is that you use some preselected standard. Using this approach guarantees that you will not be enticed into selecting an answer choice that looks right, because you are not basing your decision on how the answer choices look.

This is not meant to make you question your knowledge. Instead, it is to help you recognize the difference between your knowledge and your impressions. There's a huge difference between thinking an answer is right because of what you know, and thinking an answer is right because it looks or sounds like it should be right.

Summary: To ensure that your selection is appropriately random, make a predetermined selection from among all answer choices you have not eliminated.

Test-Taking Strategies

This section contains a list of test-taking strategies that you may find helpful as you work through the test. By taking what you know and applying logical thought, you can maximize your chances of answering any question correctly!

It is very important to realize that every question is different and every person is different: no single strategy will work on every question, and no single strategy will work for every person. That's why we've included all of them here, so you can try them out and determine which ones work best for different types of questions and which ones work best for you.

Question Strategies

READ CAREFULLY

Read the question and answer choices carefully. Don't miss the question because you misread the terms. You have plenty of time to read each question thoroughly and make sure you understand what is being asked. Yet a happy medium must be attained, so don't waste too much time. You must read carefully, but efficiently.

CONTEXTUAL CLUES

Look for contextual clues. If the question includes a word you are not familiar with, look at the immediate context for some indication of what the word might mean. Contextual clues can often give you all the information you need to decipher the meaning of an unfamiliar word. Even if you can't determine the meaning, you may be able to narrow down the possibilities enough to make a solid guess at the answer to the question.

PREFIXES

If you're having trouble with a word in the question or answer choices, try dissecting it. Take advantage of every clue that the word might include. Prefixes and suffixes can be a huge help. Usually they allow you to determine a basic meaning. Pre- means before, post- means after, pro - is positive, de- is negative. From prefixes and suffixes, you can get an idea of the general meaning of the word and try to put it into context.

HEDGE WORDS

Watch out for critical hedge words, such as *likely, may, can, sometimes, often, almost, mostly, usually, generally, rarely*, and *sometimes*. Question writers insert these hedge phrases to cover every possibility. Often an answer choice will be wrong simply because it leaves no room for exception. Be on guard for answer choices that have definitive words such as *exactly* and *always*.

SWITCHBACK WORDS

Stay alert for *switchbacks*. These are the words and phrases frequently used to alert you to shifts in thought. The most common switchback words are *but, although,* and *however*. Others include *nevertheless, on the other hand, even though, while, in spite of, despite, regardless of*. Switchback words are important to catch because they can change the direction of the question or an answer choice.

FACE VALUE

When in doubt, use common sense. Accept the situation in the problem at face value. Don't read too much into it. These problems will not require you to make wild assumptions. If you have to go beyond creativity and warp time or space in order to have an answer choice fit the question, then you should move on and consider the other answer choices. These are normal problems rooted in reality. The applicable relationship or explanation may not be readily apparent, but it is there for you to figure out. Use your common sense to interpret anything that isn't clear.

Answer Choice Strategies

ANSWER SELECTION

The most thorough way to pick an answer choice is to identify and eliminate wrong answers until only one is left, then confirm it is the correct answer. Sometimes an answer choice may immediately seem right, but be careful. The test writers will usually put more than one reasonable answer choice on each question, so take a second to read all of them and make sure that the other choices are not equally obvious. As long as you have time left, it is better to read every answer choice than to pick the first one that looks right without checking the others.

ANSWER CHOICE FAMILIES

An answer choice family consists of two (in rare cases, three) answer choices that are very similar in construction and cannot all be true at the same time. If you see two answer choices that are direct opposites or parallels, one of them is usually the correct answer. For instance, if one answer choice says that quantity x increases and another either says that quantity x decreases (opposite) or says that quantity y increases (parallel), then those answer choices would fall into the same family. An answer choice that doesn't match the construction of the answer choice family is more likely to be incorrect. Most questions will not have answer choice families, but when they do appear, you should be prepared to recognize them.

ELIMINATE ANSWERS

Eliminate answer choices as soon as you realize they are wrong, but make sure you consider all possibilities. If you are eliminating answer choices and realize that the last one you are left with is also wrong, don't panic. Start over and consider each choice again. There may be something you missed the first time that you will realize on the second pass.

AVOID FACT TRAPS

Don't be distracted by an answer choice that is factually true but doesn't answer the question. You are looking for the choice that answers the question. Stay focused on what the question is asking for so you don't accidentally pick an answer that is true but incorrect. Always go back to the question and make sure the answer choice you've selected actually answers the question and is not merely a true statement.

EXTREME STATEMENTS

In general, you should avoid answers that put forth extreme actions as standard practice or proclaim controversial ideas as established fact. An answer choice that states the "process should be used in certain situations, if..." is much more likely to be correct than one that states the "process should be discontinued completely." The first is a calm rational statement and doesn't even make a definitive, uncompromising stance, using a hedge word *if* to provide wiggle room, whereas the second choice is a radical idea and far more extreme.

BENCHMARK

As you read through the answer choices and you come across one that seems to answer the question well, mentally select that answer choice. This is not your final answer, but it's the one that will help you evaluate the other answer choices. The one that you selected is your benchmark or standard for judging each of the other answer choices. Every other answer choice must be compared to your benchmark. That choice is correct until proven otherwise by another answer choice beating it. If you find a better answer, then that one becomes your new benchmark. Once you've decided that no other choice answers the question as well as your benchmark, you have your final answer.

PREDICT THE ANSWER

Before you even start looking at the answer choices, it is often best to try to predict the answer. When you come up with the answer on your own, it is easier to avoid distractions and traps because you will know exactly what to look for. The right answer choice is unlikely to be word-for-word what you came up with, but it should be a close match. Even if you are confident that you have the right answer, you should still take the time to read each option before moving on.

General Strategies

TOUGH QUESTIONS

If you are stumped on a problem or it appears too hard or too difficult, don't waste time. Move on! Remember though, if you can quickly check for obviously incorrect answer choices, your chances of guessing correctly are greatly improved. Before you completely give up, at least try to knock out a couple of possible answers. Eliminate what you can and then guess at the remaining answer choices before moving on.

CHECK YOUR WORK

Since you will probably not know every term listed and the answer to every question, it is important that you get credit for the ones that you do know. Don't miss any questions through careless mistakes. If at all possible, try to take a second to look back over your answer selection and make sure you've selected the correct answer choice and haven't made a costly careless mistake (such as marking an answer choice that you didn't mean to mark). This quick double check should more than pay for itself in caught mistakes for the time it costs.

PACE YOURSELF

It's easy to be overwhelmed when you're looking at a page full of questions; your mind is confused and full of random thoughts, and the clock is ticking down faster than you would like. Calm down and maintain the pace that you have set for yourself. Especially as you get down to the last few minutes of the test, don't let the small numbers on the clock make you panic. As long as you are on track by monitoring your pace, you are guaranteed to have time for each question.

DON'T RUSH

It is very easy to make errors when you are in a hurry. Maintaining a fast pace in answering questions is pointless if it makes you miss questions that you would have gotten right otherwise. Test writers like to include distracting information and wrong answers that seem right. Taking a little extra time to avoid careless mistakes can make all the difference in your test score. Find a pace that allows you to be confident in the answers that you select.

KEEP MOVING

Panicking will not help you pass the test, so do your best to stay calm and keep moving. Taking deep breaths and going through the answer elimination steps you practiced can help to break through a stress barrier and keep your pace.

Final Notes

The combination of a solid foundation of content knowledge and the confidence that comes from practicing your plan for applying that knowledge is the key to maximizing your performance on test day. As your foundation of content knowledge is built up and strengthened, you'll find that the strategies included in this chapter become more and more effective in helping you quickly sift through the distractions and traps of the test to isolate the correct answer.

Now it's time to move on to the test content chapters of this book, but be sure to keep your goal in mind. As you read, think about how you will be able to apply this information on the test. If you've already seen sample questions for the test and you have an idea of the question format and style, try to come up with questions of your own that you can answer based on what you're reading. This will give you valuable practice applying your knowledge in the same ways you can expect to on test day.

Good luck and good studying!

14

Listening

The Listening test of the IELTS consists of a total of 40 questions and will last roughly 30 minutes. There will be several task types asking for either multiple choice, matching, fill-in-the-blank, or short-answer questions.

There are four types of listening situations:

1. Short social conversations between multiple speakers
2. Short social monologues from a single speaker
3. Academic conversations
4. Academic lectures

The recordings that are provided will only be provided once and may contain a variety of accents.

Tips for the Listening Section

The listening section requires you to demonstrate your ability to understand verbal information and use pragmatic understanding to interpret content, tone, and purpose.

TIP 1: LISTENING FOR BASIC COMPREHENSION

When preparing for the test, take some time to find English radio, lectures, podcasts, and videos to watch and listen to. You should pick different types of sources because during this section of the test, you will be exposed to both academic and everyday English. Practice taking mental notes of what is said and try listening for main points.

TIP 2: LISTENING FOR PRAGMATIC UNDERSTANDING

Speakers use tone and emphasis in speech to create a certain mood or to accomplish a certain goal. After you are comfortable with listening for basic comprehension, try listening for tone and try to identify a speaker's purpose. Try also to identify whether a speaker is talking more casually or informatively and if there is a particular emotion conveyed.

TIP 3: CONNECTING AND SYNTHESIZING INFORMATION

As you listen to speakers talk, you will have to connect information to form conclusions. Try to notice if two speakers make opposing points or if there is a reason behind what is said. After you listen to a sample of speech, practice summarizing and restating information, then listen again to check yourself.

Listening Skills

USE THE PICTURES

The pictures are provided to orient you to the atmosphere and environment in which the speakers are conducting their conversation. Use those pictures as much as possible. Try to put yourself in that environment. Become one of the pictured speakers and you will be able to better appreciate the conversation and what it means.

USE MULTIPLE INPUTS

The questions will be read to you at the same time they are exposed on the screen in the form of text. Take advantage of this. Use both the visual and auditory information being presented to better

understand what is being asked. Some people are better visual and some better auditory receivers of information. Since both methods of presenting questions are given, use them both to your maximum advantage.

MAIN IDEAS

Important words and main ideas in conversation are ones that will come up again and again. Listen carefully for any word or words that come up repeatedly. What words come up in nearly every statement made? These words with high frequency are likely to be in the main idea of the conversation. For example, in a conversation about class size in the business department of a college, the term "class size" is likely to appear in nearly every statement made by either speaker in the discussion.

VOICE CHANGES

On the IELTS, you are expected to be able to recognize and interpret nuances of speech. Be on the alert for any changes in voice, which might register surprise, excitement, or another emotion. If a speaker is talking in a normal monotone voice and suddenly raises their voice to a high pitch, that is a huge clue that something critical is being stated. Listen for a speaker to change their voice and understand the meaning of what they are saying.

Example:

Man: Let's go to Wal-mart.

Woman: *There's a Wal-mart in this small town?*

If the woman's statement was higher pitched, indicating surprise and shock, then she probably did not expect there to be a Wal-mart in that town.

Speakers may also place stronger stress on words that are important, which helps in understanding the focal point of a sentence or can even change sentence meaning.

Example:

Man: Did *you* play baseball over the weekend?

Woman: *We* didn't play baseball. We *watched* a baseball game over the weekend.

Example:

Man: Did you play *baseball* over the weekend?

Woman: We didn't play *baseball;* we played *tennis* instead.

In these examples, the intent of the man's question changes based on which word receives the stress.

SPECIFICS

Listen carefully for specific pieces of information. Adjectives are commonly asked about in IELTS questions. Try to remember any main adjectives that are mentioned. Pick out adjectives such as numbers, colors, or sizes.

Example:

Man: Let's go to the store and get some apples to make the pie.

Woman: How many do we need?

Man: We'll need **five** apples to make the pie.

A typical question might be about how many apples were needed.

INTERPRET

As you are listening to the conversation, put yourself in the person's shoes. Think about why someone would make a statement. You'll need to do more than just regurgitate the spoken words; you must also interpret them.

Example:

Woman: I think I'm sick with the flu.

Man: Why don't you go see the campus doctor?

Sample Question: Why did the man mention the campus doctor?

Answer: The campus doctor would be able to determine if the woman had the flu.

FIND THE HIDDEN MEANING

Look for the meaning behind a statement. When a speaker answers a question with a statement that doesn't immediately seem to answer the question, the response probably contains a hidden meaning that you will need to recognize and explain.

Man: Are you going to be ready for your presentation?

Woman: I've only got half of it finished and it's taken me five hours just to do this much. There's only an hour left before the presentation is due.

At first, the woman did not seem to answer the question the man presented. She responded with a statement that only seemed loosely related. Once you look deeper, then you can find the true meaning of what she said. If it took the woman five hours to do the first half of the presentation, then it would logically take her another five hours to do the second half. Since she only has one hour until her presentation is due, she would probably NOT be ready for the presentation. So, while an answer was not immediately visible to the man's question, when you applied logic to her response, you could find the hidden meaning.

Types of Listening Problems

TYPES OF CONVERSATIONS ON THE IELTS

On your test, you will encounter a variety of listening prompts which may include one or more speakers. These may include more academic or more informal speakers who may either agree or disagree with one another. You must be able to determine main ideas and viewpoints when encountering conversations.

ACADEMIC CONVERSATIONS

Academic conversations are conversations on a college campus between professors, students, and other campus members. You will need to be able to summarize main ideas and recall important details.

CLASS DISCUSSIONS

Class discussions are conversations in a classroom between professors and students. You will need to be able to summarize main ideas, but usually NOT need to recall important details.

ACADEMIC TALKS

Academic talks are conversations in an orientation meeting on academic courses and procedures or where a professor might discuss a variety of college topics. You will need to be able to summarize main ideas, but usually NOT need to recall important details.

LECTURES

Lectures are conversations in a classroom about academic topics. You will need to be able to summarize main ideas, and be able to answer questions such as: who, what, when, where, or why?

ACTIVE LISTENING

Although listening appears to be a passive process, it must be **active** in order to be effective. Indeed, the listener should have a **purpose** for listening. The precise purpose of listening need not be conscious in the mind of the listener. In general, there are four distinguished **intentions** of listening: comprehension, criticism, empathy, and appreciation. These intentions are often intermingled in the same act of listening. When we listen for comprehension, we are trying to understand the message the speaker is communicating. In order to listen for comprehension, we need to know the standards of grammar and punctuation in English. We also need to know the common forms of argument. We also need to have an understanding of the context in which the words are spoken so that we can understand the relationship between message and context.

LISTENING FOR THE PURPOSES OF CRITICISM

In order to listen for the purposes of criticism, one must usually also be listening for **comprehension**. It is true that in order to accurately assess the quality of a verbal communication, you will need to understand the content of the communication first. To a certain degree, however, we all apply critical listening skills to communication we have yet to fully understand. For instance, when we hear an advertisement on the radio, we know immediately that the speaker is trying to sell us something, and so we are naturally receptive or skeptical of the message, depending on our preexisting interest in the product or service. In this case, our **critical listening skills** are influencing our listening even before we have begun to comprehend the content.

LISTENING FOR CONTENT

In almost every listening situation, the audience is required to listen for **information**. A communication can only be considered effective if the message communicates the information intended by the speaker. The **feedback** issued by the audience indicates the degree to which the information has been received accurately. When the audience is required to ask for clarification or repetition of the message, it is possible that the speaker has been ineffective in delivering his or her information. Moreover, if the audience provides no verbal feedback about a delivered message, it is possible that they either do not understand any of the message or are simply not interested in it. Of course, when there is no verbal feedback it is also possible that the audience simply understands the transmitted message perfectly and requires no clarification or elaboration.

LISTENING FOR COMPREHENSION

There are five basic kinds of **intentional listening**: appreciative, therapeutic, discriminative, comprehensive, and critical. **Listening for comprehension** is probably the most familiar form of listening. Students in a classroom are engaged in listening for comprehension when they take notes during a lecture. Whenever we listen to an informative or persuasive speech in order to obtain information about a subject, we are engaged in listening for comprehension. The validity and accuracy of other forms of listening, such as critical listening and discriminative listening, depend on effective listening for comprehension. If an individual is unable to understand the message that is being presented, he or she will not be able to critique it insightfully.

ASSESSING THE CHARACTERISTICS OF THE SPEAKER

As part of the overall critique of a speech, an audience member should consider the personal **characteristics of the speaker**. For instance, the audience member might consider what he or she knew about the speaker before the speech, and then decide whether this information had any influence on his or her interpretation of the speaker's message. The audience member might also consider whether the speaker's personal presentation indicated credibility or made his or her message difficult to believe. Many times, a speaker with a good message and solid supporting materials comes across as vague and disorganized because of his or her physical appearance and vocal mannerisms. Audience members should try to distinguish between weaknesses in the speaker's message and weaknesses in the speaker's personal presentation.

ANALYZING THE MESSAGE OF THE SPEECH

When an audience member listens to a speech, he or she should be attending to three fundamental **factors**: ideas, organization, and support. The most important thing to consider is whether the speaker's main ideas are *logical and clearly expressed*. If the ideas are comprehensible, an audience member can then consider whether they have been expressed in the *logical order*, or whether the speaker has presented them in a disorganized fashion. Finally, the audience member needs to consider whether the speaker's main ideas have been adequately *supported* by argument or factual evidence. Does the speaker provide enough support for his arguments to remain credible? Is the evidence provided relevant to the main ideas of the speech?

Reading

The Academic Reading section of the IELTS consists of a total of 40 questions which will last 60 minutes.

The test will contain a variety of passage types including journals, books, newspapers, and magazines. Each source will be written for a non-specialist audience on the level of a test-taker seeking to enter an undergraduate university.

Test-takers should expect to encounter argumentative, narrative, and descriptive texts and to be prepared to interpret information from both text and non-verbal materials such as images and graphs.

Tips for the Reading Section

The reading section requires you to demonstrate your ability to find information, use basic comprehension, and read to learn.

TIP 1: READING TO FIND INFORMATION

When reading to find specific ideas, it is important to be able to **scan** or **skim** a text for a specific phrase or context. To improve your reading speed and ability to scan a text, find passages that discuss a specific topic and practice looking for main ideas quickly without taking the time to read every word or sentence.

TIP 2: BASIC COMPREHENSION

When reading for basic comprehension of a passage, you will likely be asked to identify **themes, main ideas, and vocabulary** in context. These pieces of information are most likely to be found in the first sentence of the paragraph and in introductory or conclusion paragraphs. Spend some time reading through paragraphs and short stories looking for key information.

TIP 3: READING TO LEARN

When reading to learn, one must be aware of **organization** and **presentation** of information within a passage. As you read through passages, try to identify the point of a passage, as well as whether it is speaking in an informative or persuasive manner. Keep track of important details, as some questions may require you to insert sentences that fit best in a passage. In these questions, there may be more than one answer that is technically correct, but only one that is truly the best fit.

Reading Comprehension Skills

This section is organized to introduce you to the passages that you will find on your exam. We cover the different types of passages from narrative to persuasive. Then, we move to the reason that a passage is written. As you may know, some texts are written to persuade. Other passages want to inform.

The writing devices used by writers are important to understand as you practice reading passages. The other parts of a passage we focus on are main ideas, supporting details, and themes. Then, we review making inferences and drawing conclusions. With this step-by-step guide, you will move to a higher score on your test.

Careful reading and thinking about a passage are important in every part of life. Work with this information by reading books, magazines, or newspapers. When you read carefully, you can use this information for other passages. With practice you will strengthen your skills for the future.

TYPES OF PASSAGES

A **narrative** passage is a story that can be fiction or nonfiction (i.e., false or true). To be a narrative, the passage must have a few things. First, the text must have a plot (i.e., an order of events). Some narratives are written in a clear order, but this is not necessary. If the narrative is good, then you will find these events interesting. Second, a narrative has characters. These characters can be people, animals, or even lifeless items. As long as they play in the plot, they are characters. Third, a narrative passage often has figurative language. This is a tool that authors use to stir the imagination of readers with comparisons or comments. For example, a metaphor is a comparison between two things without using the words *like* or *as*. *He stood like a king* is not an example of a metaphor. *The moon was a frosty snowball* is an example of a metaphor. In reality, this is not true. Yet, the comparison creates a vivid mental image for readers.

An **expository** passage aims to inform or teach readers. The passage is nonfiction and usually centers around an easily explained topic. Often, an expository passage has helpful organizing words such as *first*, *next*, *for example*, and *therefore*. These words let readers know where they are in the passage. While expository passages don't need to have difficult vocabulary and fancy writing, they may be improved by them. Yet this can make it difficult to pay attention to an expository passage. Expository passages are not always on topics you will find interesting. Also, writers focus more on clarity and precision than with keeping the reader's interest. By careful reading, you will establish a good habit of focus when you read an expository passage.

A **technical** passage is written to describe a complicated thing or action. Technical writing is common in medical and technology fields. In those fields, ideas of mathematics, science, and engineering need to be explained simply and clearly. A technical passage usually proceeds in a step-by-step order to help with understanding the passage. Technical passages often have clear headings and subheadings. These headings act like the organizing words in an expository passage: they let readers know where they are in a passage. Also, you will find that these passages divide sections by numbers or letters. Many technical passages look more like an outline than the paragraphs that you are reading right now. Depending on the audience, the amount of difficult vocabulary will change in a technical passage. Some technical passages try to stay away from language that readers will have to look up. However, some difficult vocabulary has to be used for writers to share their message.

A **persuasive** passage is written to change the minds of readers so that they agree with the author. The purpose of the passage may be very clear or very difficult to find. A persuasive passage wants to make an acceptable argument and win the trust of the reader. In some cases, a persuasive passage will be similar to an informative passage. Both passages make an argument and offer supporting details. However, a persuasive passage is more likely to appeal to the reader's feelings and make arguments based on opinions. Persuasive passages may not describe other points of view. So, when they do show other points of view, they may show favoritism to one side.

Persuasive passages will focus on one **main argument** and make many **minor arguments** (i.e., arguments that help the main argument) along the way. If you are going to accept the main argument, then you need to accept the minor arguments. So, the main argument will only be as strong as the minor arguments. These arguments should be rooted in fact and experience, not opinions. The best persuasive passages give enough supporting detail to back up arguments without confusing readers. Remember that a fact must be open to independent verification (i.e., the fact must be something that can be backed up by someone else). Also, statistics (i.e., data or figures are collected for study) are helpful only when they look at other choices. For example, a statistic on the number of bicycles sold would only be useful if it was taken over a limited time period and in a specific area. Good readers are careful with statistics because statistics can show what the author wants us to see. Or, they can hide what the author doesn't want to show. The writers of your test know that their passages will be met by questioning readers. So, your skill at questioning what you read will be a help in your exam.

Opinions come from how we feel and what we think. Persuasive writers often try to appeal to the emotions (i.e., use or influence someone's feelings) of readers to make their arguments. You should always ask questions about this approach. You should ask questions because an author can pull you into accepting something that you don't want to accept. Sometimes these appeals can be used fairly. For example, some subjects cannot be totally addressed without an appeal to a reader's feelings. Think about an article on drunk driving. Some examples in the article will alarm or sadden readers because of the terrible outcome.

On the other hand, appeals to feelings are unacceptable when they try to **mislead** readers. For example, a presidential candidate (i.e., someone running for president) says that he/she cares about the country. The candidate pushes you to make a connection. You care about the country as well and have positive feelings toward it. The candidate wants you to connect your positive feelings about the country with your thoughts about him or her. If you make more connections with the candidate, then you are likely to vote for him or her. Also, the person running for president hints that other candidates do not care about the country.

Another common and unacceptable appeal to feelings is the use of **loaded language**. Calling a religious person a *fanatic* or a person interested in the environment a *tree hugger* are examples of loaded language.

> **Review Video: Appeal to Emotion**
> Visit mometrix.com/academy and enter code: 163442

ORGANIZATION OF THE PASSAGE

The way a passage is organized can help readers to understand the author's purpose and conclusions. There are many ways to organize a passage, and each one has an important use.

Some nonfiction texts are organized to present a **problem** followed by a **solution**. For this type of passage, the problem is explained before the solution is given. When the problem is well known, the solution may be given in a few sentences at the beginning. Other passages may focus on the solution, and the problem will be talked about a few times. Some passages will outline many solutions to a problem. This will leave you to choose among the possible solutions. If authors have loyalty to one solution, they may not describe some of the other solutions. Be careful with the author's plan when reading a problem-solution passage. When you know the author's point of view, you can make a better judgment of the solution.

Sometimes authors will organize information clearly for you to follow and locate the information. However, this is not always the case with passages in an exam. Two common ways to order a passage are cause and effect and chronological order. When using **chronological order** (i.e., a plan that moves in order from the first step to the last), the author gives information in the order that the event happened. For example, biographies are written in chronological order. The person's birth and childhood are first. Their adult life is next. The events leading up to the person's death are last.

In **cause and effect**, an author shows one thing that makes something else happen. For example, if one were to go to bed very late and wake up very early, he/she would be tired in the morning. The cause is lack of sleep, with the effect of being tired the next day.

Finding the cause-and-effect relationships in a passage can be tricky. Often, these relationships come with certain words or terms. When authors use words like *because, since, in order,* and *so,* they are describing a cause and effect relationship. Think about the sentence: *He called her because he needed the homework.* This is a simple causal relationship. The cause was his need for the homework, and the effect was his phone call. However, not all cause and effect relationships are marked like this. Think about the sentences: *He called her. He needed the homework.* When the cause-and-effect relationship does not come with a keyword, the relationship can be known by asking why. For example, He called her: *why?* The answer is in the next sentence: He needed the homework.

When authors try to change the minds of readers, they may use cause-and-effect relationships. However, these relationships should not always be taken at face value. To read a persuasive essay well, you need to judge the cause-and-effect relationships. For example, imagine an author wrote the following: *The parking deck has not been making money because people want to ride their bikes.* The relationship is clear: the cause is that people want to ride their bikes. The effect is that the parking deck has not been making money. However, you should look at this argument again. Maybe there are other reasons that the parking deck was not a success: a bad economy, too many costs, etc.

Many passages follow the **compare-and-contrast** model. In this model, the similarities and differences between two ideas or things are reviewed. A review of the similarities between ideas is called comparison. In a perfect comparison, the author shows ideas or things in the same way. If authors want to show the similarities between football and baseball, they can list the equipment and rules for each game. Think about the similarities as they appear in the passage and take note of any differences.

Careful thinking about ideas and conclusions can seem like a difficult task. You can make this task easy by understanding the basic parts of ideas and writing skills. Looking at the way that ideas link to others is a good way to begin. Sometimes authors will write about two opposing ideas. Other times, an author will support a topic, and another author will argue against the topic. The review of these rival ideas is known as **contrast**. In contrast, all ideas should be presented clearly. If the author does favor a side, you need to read carefully to find how the author shows or hides this favoritism. Also, as you read the passage, you should write out how one side views the other.

PURPOSES FOR WRITING

To be a careful reader, pay attention to the author's **position** and purpose. Even passages that seem fair and equal—like textbooks—have a position or bias (i.e., the author is unfair or inaccurate with opposing ideas). Readers need to take these positions into account when considering the author's message. Authors who appeal to feelings or favor one side of an argument make their position clear. Authors' positions may be found in what they write and in what they don't write. Normally, you would want to review other passages on the same topic to understand the author's position. However, you are in the middle of an exam. So, look for language and arguments that show a position.

Sometimes, finding the **purpose** of an author is easier than finding his or her position. In most cases, the author has no interest in hiding his or her purpose. A passage for *entertainment* will be written to please readers. Most stories are written to entertain. However, they can inform or persuade. *Informative* texts are easy to recognize. The most difficult purpose of a text to determine is *persuasion*. In persuasion, the author wants to make the purpose hard to find. When you learn that the author wants to persuade, you should be skeptical of the argument. Persuasive passages try to establish an entertaining tone and hope to amuse you into agreement. On the other hand, an informative tone may be used to seem fair and equal to all sides.

An author's purpose is clear often in the **organization** of the text (such as section headings in bold font points for an informative passage). However, you may not have this organization in your passages. So, if authors make their main idea clear from the beginning, then their likely purpose is to *inform*. If the author makes a main argument and gives minor arguments for support, then the purpose is probably to *persuade*. If the author tells a story, then his or her purpose is most likely to *entertain*. If the author wants to gain your attention more than to persuade or inform, then his or her purpose is most likely to entertain. You must judge authors by how well they achieve their purpose. In other words, think about the type of passage (technical, persuasive, etc.) that the author has written and whether the author has followed the demands of the passage type.

The author's purpose will influence his or her writing approach and the reader's reaction. In a **persuasive essay**, the author wants to prove something to readers. There are several important marks of persuasive writing. Opinion given as fact is one mark. When authors try to persuade readers, they give their opinions as if they were facts. Readers must be on guard for statements that sound like facts but cannot be tested. Another mark of persuasive writing is the appeal to feelings. An author will try to play with the feelings of readers by appealing to their ideas of what is right and wrong. When an author uses strong language to excite the reader's feelings, then the author may want to persuade. Many times, a persuasive passage will give an unfair explanation of other sides, or simply not show the other sides.

An **informative passage** is written to teach readers. Informative passages are almost always nonfiction. The purpose of an informative passage is to share information in the clearest way. In an informative passage, you may have a *thesis statement* (an argument on the topic of a passage that is later proven). A thesis statement is a sentence that normally comes at the end of the first paragraph. Authors of informative passages are likely to place more importance on clarity. Informative passages do not normally appeal to the feelings. They often contain facts and figures, and almost never include the author's opinion. However, you should know that there can be a bias in the facts. Sometimes, a persuasive passage can be like an informative passage. This is true when authors give their ideas as if they were facts.

Entertainment passages describe real or imagined people, places, and events. Entertainment passages are often stories or poems. So, figurative language is a common part of these passages. Often, an entertainment passage appeals to the imagination and feelings. Authors may persuade or inform in an entertainment passage. Or, an entertainment passage may cause readers to think differently about a subject.

When authors want to **share feelings,** they may use strong language. Authors may share feelings about a moment of great pain or happiness. Other times, authors will try to persuade readers by sharing feelings. Some phrases like *I felt* and *I sense* hint that the author is sharing feelings. Authors may share stories of deep pain or great joy. You must not be influenced by these stories. You need to keep some distance to judge the author's argument.

Almost all writing is descriptive. In one way or another, authors try to describe events, ideas, or people. But some texts are concerned only with **description**. A descriptive passage focuses on a single subject and seeks to explain the subject clearly. Descriptive passages contain many adjectives and adverbs (words that give a complete picture for you to imagine). Normally, a descriptive passage is informative. Yet, the passage may be persuasive or entertaining.

WRITING DEVICES

Authors will use different writing devices to make their message clear for readers. One of those devices is comparison and contrast. As mentioned above, when authors show how two things are alike, they are **comparing** them. When authors describe how two things are different, they are **contrasting** them. The compare and contrast passage is a common part of nonfiction. Comparisons are known by certain words or phrases: *both, same, like, too,* and *as well.* Contrasts may have words or phrases like *but, however, on the other hand, instead,* and *yet.* Of course, comparisons and contrasts may be understood without using those words or phrases. A single sentence may compare and contrast. Think about the sentence *Brian and Sheila love ice cream, but Brian loves vanilla and Sheila loves strawberry.* In one sentence, the author has described both a similarity (love of ice cream) and a difference (favorite flavor).

> **Review Video: Compare and Contrast**
> Visit mometrix.com/academy and enter code: 798319

Another regular writing device is **cause and effect**. A cause is an act or event that makes something happen. An effect is what comes from the cause. A cause and effect relationship is not always easy to find. Several words and phrases can be used to show causes: *since, because,* and *due to.* Words and phrases that show effects include *consequently, therefore, this lead(s) to, as a result.* For example, a cause and effect sentence is: *Because the sky was clear, Ron did not bring an umbrella.* The cause is the clear sky, and the effect is that Ron did not bring an umbrella. Readers may find that the cause and effect relationship is not clear. For example, *He was late and missed the meeting.* This does not have any words that show cause or effect. Yet, the sentence still has a cause (he was late) and an effect (he missed the meeting).

Remember the chance for a **single cause** to have many effects. For example, a single-cause sentence is: *Because you left your homework on the table, your dog eats the homework.* The single cause of leaving homework on the table can have many effects: (1) You fail your homework. (2) Your parents do not let you see your friends. (3) You miss out on the new movie. (4) You miss holding the hand of an important person.

Also, a **single effect** can have many causes. For example, a single-effect sentence is: *Alan has a fever.* This fever can have multiple causes: 1) An unexpected cold front came through the area. (2) Alan forgot to take his multi-vitamin.

An effect can also become the cause of another effect. This is known as a **cause and effect chain**. For example: *As a result of her hatred for not doing work, Lynn got ready for her exam.* This led to her passing her test with high marks. Hence, her resume was accepted, and her application was also accepted.

Often, authors use analogies to add meaning to their passages. An **analogy** is a comparison of two things. The words in the analogy are connected by a relationship. Look at this analogy: *moo is to cow as quack is to duck.* This analogy compares the sound that a cow makes with the sound that a duck makes. What could you do if the word *quack* was not given? Well, you could finish the analogy if you know the connection between *moo* and *cow*. Relationships for analogies include synonyms, antonyms, part to whole, definition, and actor to action.

Point of view has an important influence on a passage. A passage's point of view is how the author or a character sees or thinks about things. A point of view influences the events of a passage, the meetings among characters, and the ending to the story. For example, two characters watch a child ride a bike. Character one watches outside. Character two watches from inside a house. Both see the same event, yet they are around different noises, sights, and smells. Character one may see different things that happen outside that character two cannot see from inside. Also, point of view can be influenced by past events and beliefs. For example, if character one loves bikes, then she will remember how proud she is of the child. If character two is afraid of riding bikes, then he may not remember the event or may fear for the child's safety.

In fiction, the two main points of view are **first person** and **third person**. The *narrator* is the person who tells a story's events. The *protagonist* is the main character of a story. If the narrator is the protagonist in a story, then the story is written in first-person. In first person, the author writes from the view of *I*. Third-person point of view is the most common among stories. With third person, authors refer to each character by using *he* or *she* and the narrator is not involved in the story. In third-person omniscient, the narrator is not a character in the story and tells the story of all of the characters at the same time.

> **Review Video: Point of View**
> Visit mometrix.com/academy and enter code: 383336

Transitional words and phrases are devices that guide readers through a passage. You may know the common transitions, though you may not have thought about how they are used. Some transitional phrases (*after, before, during, in the middle of*) give information about time. Some hint that an example is about to be given (*for example, in fact, for instance*). Writers use transitions to compare (*also, likewise*) and contrast (*however, but, yet*). Transitional words and phrases can point to addition (*and, also, furthermore, moreover*) and understood relationships (*if, then, therefore, as a result, since*). Finally, transitional words and phrases can separate the chronological steps (*first, second, last*).

> **Review Video: Transitional Words and Phrases**
> Visit mometrix.com/academy and enter code: 197796

UNDERSTANDING A PASSAGE

One of the most important skills in reading comprehension is finding **topics** and **main ideas.** There is a small difference between these two. The topic is the *subject* of a passage (what the passage is all about). The main idea is the most important *argument* being made by the author. The topic is shared in a few words while the main idea needs a full sentence to be understood. As an example, a short passage might have the topic of penguins, and the main idea could be written as *Penguins are different from other birds in many ways.*

In most nonfiction writing, the topic and the main idea will be stated clearly. Sometimes, they will come in a sentence at the very beginning or end of the passage. When you want to know the topic, you frequently find it in the first sentence of each paragraph. A body paragraph's first sentence is often--but not always--the topic sentence. The topic sentence gives you a summary of the ideas in the paragraph. You may find that the topic or main idea is not given clearly. So, you must read every sentence of the passage. Then, try to come up with an overall idea from each sentence.

Note: A thesis statement is not the same as the main idea. The main idea gives a brief, general summary of a text. The thesis statement gives a clear idea on an issue that is backed up with evidence.

> **Review Video: Topics and Main Ideas**
> Visit mometrix.com/academy and enter code: 407801

PASSAGE STRUCTURE FOR NON-NARRATIVE PASSAGES

TITLE

Centered on the page, the title's main words are capitalized (articles, prepositions, and infinitives are not capitalized in a title). The title may have quotation marks, or it may be underlined or italicized. The title has a few words that hint at the subject of the paper and catch the reader's interest.

INTRODUCTION

An introduction summarizes the passage and the thesis statement. The purpose of the introduction is to grab the reader's attention. To do this, authors may use a quote, question, or strong opinion. Some authors choose to use an interesting description or puzzling statement. Also, authors use the introduction to explain their reason for writing.

BODY PARAGRAPH

Following the introduction, body paragraphs are used to explain the thesis statement. A body paragraph has a topic sentence, typically the first sentence. In these paragraphs, there is evidence that helps the argument of the paragraph. Also, the author may give commentary on the evidence. Be careful because this commentary can be filled with bias.

The topic sentence gives the paragraph's subject and the main idea. The rest of the body paragraph should be linked to the topic sentence. Again, the topic sentence should be supported with facts, details, and examples.

The topic sentence is general and covers the ideas in a body paragraph. Sometimes, the topic sentence may be implied (i.e., the sentence is not stated directly by the author). Also, the topic sentence shows the connections among the supporting details.

CONCLUSION

The conclusion should provide a summary on the passage. New material is not given in the conclusion. The conclusion is the final paragraph that may have a call to action (something the writer wants readers to do) or a question for the reader to think about.

The main idea is the umbrella argument of a passage. So, **supporting details** back up the main idea. To show that a main idea is correct, authors add details that prove their idea. All passages contain details. However, they are supporting details when they help an argument in the passage. Supporting details are found in informative and persuasive texts. Sometimes they will come with terms like *for example* or *for instance*. Or, they will be numbered with terms like *first*, *second*, and *last*. You should think about how the author's supporting details back up his or her main idea. Supporting details can be factual yet biased toward the author's main idea. Sometimes supporting details can seem helpful. However, they may be useless when they are based on opinions.

> **Review Video: Supporting Details**
> Visit mometrix.com/academy and enter code: 396297

An example of a main idea is: *Giraffes live in the Serengeti of Africa.* A supporting detail about giraffes could be: *A giraffe in the Serengeti benefits from a long neck by reaching twigs and leaves on tall trees.* The main idea gives the general idea that the text is about giraffes. The supporting detail gives a clear fact about how the giraffes eat.

A **theme** is an issue, an idea, or a question raised by a passage. For example, a theme of *Cinderella* is determination as Cinderella serves her stepsisters and stepmother. Passages may have many themes, so be careful to find only themes that you are asked to find. One common mark of themes is that they give more questions than answers. Authors try to push readers to consider themes in other ways. You can find themes by asking about the general problems that the passage is addressing. A good way to find a theme is to begin reading with a question in mind (e.g., How does this passage use the theme of love?) and to look for answers to that question.

> **Review Video: Theme**
> Visit mometrix.com/academy and enter code: 732074

EVALUATING A PASSAGE

When you read informational passages, you need to make a conclusion from the author's writing. You can **identify a logical conclusion** (find a conclusion that makes sense) to know whether you agree or disagree with an author. Coming to this conclusion is like making an inference: you combine the information from the passage with what you already know. From the passage's information and your knowledge, you can come to a conclusion that makes sense. One way to have a conclusion that makes sense is to take notes of all the author's points. When the notes are organized, they may point to the logical conclusion. Another way to reach conclusions is to ask if the author's passage raises any helpful questions. Sometimes you will be able to draw many conclusions from a passage. Yet, these may be conclusions that were never imagined by the author. Therefore, find reasons in the passage for the conclusions that you make.

> **Review Video: Identifying Logical Conclusions**
> Visit mometrix.com/academy and enter code: 281653

Text evidence is the information that supports a main argument or minor argument. This evidence, or proof, can lead you to a conclusion. Information used as text evidence is clear, descriptive, and full of facts. Supporting details give evidence to back up an argument.

For example, a passage may state that winter occurs during opposite months in the Northern hemisphere (north of the equator) and Southern hemisphere (south of the equator). Text evidence for this claim may include a list of countries where winter occurs in opposite months. Also, you may be given reasons that winter occurs at different times of the year in these hemispheres (such as the tilt of the earth as it rotates around the sun).

A text is **credible**, or believable, when the author is knowledgeable and fair. The author's motivations for writing the passage have an important part in judging the credibility of the passage. For example, passages written about a professional soccer game by a sports reporter and an average fan will have different levels of credibility.

A reader should always draw **conclusions** from passages. Sometimes conclusions are implied (i.e., information that is assumed) from written information. Other times the information is **stated directly** within the passage. You should try to draw conclusions from information stated in a passage. Furthermore, you should always read through the entire passage before drawing conclusions. Readers often expect the author's conclusions at the beginning or the end of the passage. However, many texts do not follow this format.

Implications are things that the author does not say directly, but you can assume from what the author does say. For example: *I stepped outside and opened my umbrella. By the time I got to work, the cuffs of my pants were soaked.* The author never says that it is raining. However, you can conclude that this information is implied. Conclusions from implications must be well supported by the passage. To draw a conclusion, you should have many pieces of proof. If you have only one piece of evidence, then you need to be sure that there is no other possible explanation than your conclusion. Practice drawing conclusions from implications in real life events to improve your skills.

Outlining the information in a passage should be a familiar skill to readers. A good outline will show the pattern of the passage and lead to better conclusions. A common outline lists the main ideas of the passage in the order that they come. Then, beneath each main idea, you can list the minor ideas and details. An outline does not need to include every detail from the passage. However, the outline should show everything that is important to the argument.

Another helpful tool is **summarizing** information. This process is similar to creating an outline. First, a summary should define the main idea of the passage. The summary should have the most important supporting details or arguments. Summaries can be unclear or wrong because they do not stay true to the information in the passage. A helpful summary should have the same message as the passage.

Ideas from a passage can be organized using **graphic organizers**. A graphic organizer reduces information to a few key points. A graphic organizer like a timeline may have an event listed for each date on the timeline. However, an outline may have an event listed under a key point that happens in the passage.

Make a graphic organizer that works best for you. Whatever helps you remember information from a passage is what you need to use. A spider-map is another example. This map takes a main idea from the story and places it in a bubble. From one main idea bubble, you put supporting points that connect to the main idea. A Venn diagram groups information as separate or connected with some overlap.

Review Video: <u>Graphic Organizers</u>
Visit mometrix.com/academy and enter code: 665513

Paraphrasing is another method that you can use to understand a passage. To paraphrase, you put what you have read into your own words. Or, you can *translate* what the author shared into your words by including as many details as you can.

RESPONDING TO A PASSAGE

One part of being a good reader is making predictions. A **prediction** is a guess about what will happen next. Readers make predictions from what they have read and what they already know. For example: *Staring at the computer screen in shock, Kim reached for the glass of water.* The sentence leaves you to think that she is not looking at the glass. So, you may guess that Kim is going to knock over the glass. Yet in the next sentence you may read that Kim does not knock over the glass. As you have more information, be ready for your predictions to change.

Review Video: <u>Predictions</u>
Visit mometrix.com/academy and enter code: 437248

Test-taking tip: To respond to questions that ask about predictions, your answer should come from the passage.

You will be asked to understand text that gives ideas without stating them directly. An **inference** is something that is implied but not stated directly by the author. For example: *After the final out of the inning, the fans were filled with joy and rushed the field.* From this sentence, you can infer that the fans were watching baseball and their team won. You should not use information outside of the passage before making inferences. As you practice making inferences, you will find that they need all of your attention.

Review Video: <u>Inference</u>
Visit mometrix.com/academy and enter code: 379203

Test-taking tip: When asked about inferences, look for **context clues**. Context is what surrounds the words and sentences, adding explanation or information to an unknown piece. An answer can be *true* but not *correct*. The context clues will help you find the answer that is best. When asked for the implied meaning of a statement, you should locate the statement first. Then, read the context around the statement. Finally, look for an answer with a similar phrase.

For your exam, you must be able to find a text's **sequence** (i.e., the order that things happen). When the sequence is very important to the author, the passage comes with signal words: *first, then, next,* and *last*. However, a sequence can be implied. For example, *He walked through the garden and gave water and fertilizer to the plants.* Clearly, the man did not walk through the garden at the beginning. First, he found water. Then, he collected fertilizer. Next, he walked through the garden. Finally, he gave water and fertilizer to the plants. Passages do not always come in a clear sequence. Sometimes

30

they begin at the end. Or, they can begin halfway through and then start over at the beginning. You can strengthen your understanding of the passage by taking notes to understand the sequence.

Dual passages, or comparative essays, give two passages from authors with different points of view. The format of the two passages will change with each exam. For example, the author of the first passage may give an idea from his or her point of view. Then, the author of the second passage gives an argument against the first passage. Other dual passages will give a topic in the first passage. Then the second passage will support or provide explanation for the topic in the first passage.

You may see that the questions ask about passage one, passage two, and both passages. No matter the length or kind of passages, you should read them in order (read Passage 1 first, then move on to Passage 2). However, if your time is limited, you can read passage 1 first and answer all of the questions for passage 1. Then, read passage 2 and answer the remaining questions.

Building a Vocabulary

Learning the basics of language is helpful in understanding what you read. **Structural analysis** means to break a word into pieces to find its definition. Parts of a word include prefixes, suffixes, and root words. Knowing the meanings of these parts can help you understand the definition of a difficult word.

The main part of a word is known as the root. Prefixes are common letter combinations at the beginning of words. Suffixes are common letter combinations at the ends of words. In pieces, a word looks like this: prefix + root word + suffix. First, look at the individual definitions of the root word, prefix, and/or suffix. Then, see how they add to the root. You can use knowledge of a prefix's and/or suffix's definition to determine a close definition of the word. For example, if you don't know the definition of *uninspired* you may be able to figure it out because you know that *un-* means 'not.' Thus, the full word means *not inspired*. Learning the common prefixes and suffixes can help you define difficult words.

> **Review Video: <u>Determining Word Meanings</u>**
> Visit mometrix.com/academy and enter code: 894894

Below is a list of common prefixes and their meanings:

PREFIXES FOR NUMBERS

Prefix	Definition	Examples
bi-	two	bisect, biennial, bicycle
mono-	one, single	monogamy, monologue, monopoly
poly-	many	polymorphous, polygamous, polygon
semi-	half, partly	semicircle, semicolon, semiannually
uni-	one	uniform, unity, unanimous

PREFIXES FOR TIME, DIRECTION, AND SPACE

Prefix	Definition	Examples
a-	in, on, of, up, to	abed, afoot
ab-	from, away, off	abdicate, abjure
ad-	to, toward	advance, adventure
ante-	before, previous	antecedent, antedate
anti-	against, opposing	antipathy, antidote
cata-	down, away, thoroughly	catastrophe, cataclysm
circum-		circumspect, circumference
com-	with, together, very	commotion, complicate
contra-	against, opposing	contradict, contravene
de-	from	depart
dia-	through, across, apart	diameter, diagnose
dis-	away, off, down, not	dissent, disappear
epi-	upon	epilogue
ex-	out	extract, excerpt
hypo-	under, beneath	hypodermic, hypothesis
inter-	among, between	intercede, interrupt
intra-	within	intramural, intrastate
ob-	against, opposing	objection
per-	through	perceive, permit
peri-	around	periscope, perimeter
post-	after, following	postpone, postscript
pre-	before, previous	prevent, preclude
pro-	forward, in place of	propel, pronoun
retro-	back, backward	retrospect, retrograde
sub-	under, beneath	subjugate, substitute
super-	above, extra	supersede, supernumerary
trans-	across, beyond, over	transact, transport
ultra-	beyond, excessively	ultramodern, ultrasonic

NEGATIVE PREFIXES

Prefix	Definition	Examples
a-	without, lacking	atheist, agnostic
in-	not, opposing	incapable, ineligible
non-	not	nonentity, nonsense
un-	not, reverse of	unhappy, unlock

EXTRA PREFIXES

Prefix	Definition	Examples
belli-	war, warlike	bellicose
bene-	well, good	benefit, benefactor
equi-	equal	equivalent, equilibrium
for-	away, off, from	forget, forswear
fore-	previous	foretell, forefathers
homo-	same, equal	homogenized, homonym
hyper-	excessive, over	hypercritical, hypertension
in-	in, into	intrude, invade
magn-	large	magnitude, magnify
mal-	bad, poorly, not	malfunction, malpractice
mis-	bad, poorly, not	misspell, misfire
mor-	death	mortality, mortuary
neo-	new	Neolithic, neoconservative
omni-	all, everywhere	omniscient, omnivore
ortho-	right, straight	orthogonal, orthodox
over-	above	overbearing, oversight
pan-	all, entire	panorama, pandemonium
para-	beside, beyond	parallel, paradox
phil-	love, like	philosophy, philanthropic
prim-	first, early	primitive, primary
re-	backward, again	revoke, recur
sym-	with, together	sympathy, symphony
vis-	to see	visage, visible

34

Below is a list of common suffixes and their meanings:

ADJECTIVE SUFFIXES

Suffix	Definition	Examples
-able (-ible)	capable of being	toler*able*, ed*ible*
-esque	in the style of, like	picturesque, grotesque
-ful	filled with, marked by	thankful, zestful
-ic	make, cause	terrific, beatific
-ish	suggesting, like	churlish, childish
-less	lacking, without	hopeless, countless
-ous	marked by, given to	religious, riotous

NOUN SUFFIXES

Suffix	Definition	Examples
-acy	state, condition	accuracy, privacy
-ance	act, condition, fact	acceptance, vigilance
-ard	one that does excessively	drunkard, sluggard
-ation	action, state, result	occupation, starvation
-dom	state, rank, condition	serfdom, wisdom
-er (-or)	office, action	teach*er*, elevat*or*, hon*or*
-ess	feminine	waitress, duchess
-hood	state, condition	manhood, statehood
-ion	action, result, state	union, fusion
-ism	act, manner, doctrine	barbarism, socialism
-ist	worker, follower	monopolist, socialist
-ity (-ty)	state, quality, condition	acid*ity*, civil*ity*, twen*ty*
-ment	result, action	refreshment
-ness	quality, state	greatness, tallness
-ship	position	internship, statesmanship
-sion (-tion)	state, result	revi*sion*, expedi*tion*
-th	act, state, quality	warmth, width
-tude	quality, state, result	magnitude, fortitude

VERB SUFFIXES

Suffix	Definition	Examples
-ate	having, showing	separate, desolate
-en	cause to be, become	deepen, strengthen
-fy	make, cause to have	glorify, fortify
-ize	cause to be, treat with	sterilize, mechanize

Review Video: English Root Words
Visit mometrix.com/academy and enter code: 896380

There is more to a word than the dictionary definition. The **denotative** meaning of a word is the actual meaning found in a dictionary. For example, a house and a home are places where people live. The **connotative meaning** is what comes to mind when you think of a word. For example, a house may be a simple, solid building. Yet, a home may be a comfortable, welcoming place where a

Mometrix

family dwells. Most nonfiction is fact-based with no use of figurative language. So, you can assume that the writer will use denotative meanings. In fiction, drama, and poetry, the author may use the connotative meaning. Use context clues to know if the author is using the denotative or connotative meaning of a word.

Review Video: Denotation and Connotation
Visit mometrix.com/academy and enter code: 310092

Readers of all levels will find new words in passages. The best way to define a word in **context** is to think about the words that are around the unknown word. For example, nouns that you don't know may be followed by examples that give a definition. Think about this example: *Dave arrived at the party in hilarious garb: a leopard-print shirt, buckskin pants, and tennis shoes.* If you didn't know the meaning of 'garb,' you could read the examples (leopard-print shirt, buckskin pants, and tennis shoes) and know that *garb* means *clothing*. Examples will not always be this clear. Try another example: *Parsley, lemon, and flowers were just a few of items he used as garnishes.* The word *garnishes* is explained by parsley, lemon, and flowers. From this one sentence, you may infer that the items are used for decoration. Are they decorating a food plate or an ice table with meat? You would need the other sentences in the paragraph to know for sure.

Review Video: Context
Visit mometrix.com/academy and enter code: 613660

Also, you can use contrasts to define an unfamiliar word in context. In many sentences, authors will not describe the unfamiliar word directly. Instead, they will describe the opposite of the unfamiliar word. So, you are given some information that will bring you closer to defining the word. For example: *Despite his intelligence, Hector's bad posture made him look obtuse.* *Despite* means that Hector's posture is at odds with his intelligence. The author explains that Hector's posture does not prove his intelligence. So, *obtuse* must mean *unintelligent.* Another example: *Even with the horrible weather, we were beatific about our trip to Alaska.* The weather is described as *horrible.* So, *beatific* must mean something positive.

Sometimes, there will be very few context clues to help you define an unknown word. When this happens, **substitution** is a helpful tool. First, try to think of some synonyms for the words. Then, use those synonyms in place of the unknown words. If the passage makes sense, then the substitution has given some information about the unknown word. For example: *Frank's admonition rang in her ears as she climbed the mountain.* If you don't know the definition of *admonition*, try some substitutions: *vow, promise, advice, complaint,* or *compliment.* These words hint that an *admonition* is some sort of message. Once in a while substitution can get you a precise definition.

Usually you can define an unfamiliar word by looking at the descriptive words in the context. For example: *Fred dragged the recalcitrant boy, kicking and screaming, up the stairs.* The words *dragged, kicking,* and *screaming* all hint that the boy hates going up the stairs. So, you may deduce that *recalcitrant* means something like unwilling or protesting. In this example, an unfamiliar adjective was identified. Contrasts do not always give detailed information about the unknown word. However, they do give you some clues to understand it.

Description is used more to define an unfamiliar noun than unfamiliar adjectives. For example: *Don's wrinkled frown and constantly shaking fist labeled him as a curmudgeon.* Don is described as

36

Copyright © Mometrix Media. You have been licensed one copy of this document for personal use only. Any other reproduction or redistribution is strictly prohibited. All rights reserved.

having a *wrinkled frown* and *constantly shaking fist*. This hints that a *curmudgeon* must be a grumpy, old man.

Many words have more than one **definition**. So you may not know how the word is being used in a sentence. For example, the verb *cleave* can mean *join* or *separate*. When you see this word, you need to pick the definition that makes the most sense. For example: *The birds cleaved together as they flew from the oak tree.* The use of the word *together* hints that *cleave* is being used to mean *join*. Another example: *Hermione's knife cleaved the bread cleanly.* A knife cannot join bread together. So, the word must hint at separation. Learning the purpose of a word with many meanings needs the same tricks as defining an unknown word. Look for context clues and try substituting words.

To learn more from a passage, you need to understand how words connect to each other. This is done with understanding **synonyms** (e.g., words that mean the same thing) and **antonyms** (e.g., the opposite meaning of a word). For example, *dry* and *arid* are synonyms. However, *dry* and *wet* are antonyms. There are pairs of words in English that can be called synonyms, yet they have somewhat different definitions. For example, *friendly* and *collegial* can be used to describe a warm, close relationship. So, you would be correct to call them synonyms. However, *collegial* (linked to *colleague*) is used for professional or academic relationships. *Friendly* is not linked to professional or academic relationships.

Words should not be called synonyms when their differences are too great. For example, *hot* and *warm* are not synonyms because their meanings are too different. How do you know when two words are synonyms? First, try to replace one word for the other word. Then, be sure that the meaning of the sentence has not changed. Replacing *warm* for *hot* in a sentence gives a different meaning. *Warm* and *hot* may seem close in meaning. Yet *warm* means that the temperature is normal, while *hot* means that the temperature is very high.

Antonyms are words with opposite meanings. *Light* and *dark*, *up* and *down*, *right* and *left*, *good* and *bad* are sets of antonyms. However, there is a difference between antonyms and pairs of words that are different. *Black* and *gray* are not antonyms, because *black* is not the opposite of *gray*. On the other hand, *black* and *white* are antonyms. Not every word has an antonym. For example, many nouns do not have an antonym. What would be the antonym of *chair*?

During your exam, the questions about antonyms are likely to be about adjectives. Remember that adjectives are words that describe a noun. Some common adjectives include *red*, *fast*, *skinny*, and *sweet*. From these four adjectives, *red* is the one that does not have an antonym.

Review Video: Synonyms and Antonyms
Visit mometrix.com/academy and enter code: 105612

Writing

You will have 60 minutes to complete two writing tasks during the writing section. The **first task** will involve reviewing visual information from a diagram, chart, or table, and provide an explanation of the information. The response should be at least 150 words with no maximum limit. The test-taker should reserve more time for the second task, as it should take more time to complete. In the **second task**, the test-taker is asked to write a semi-formal discussion of a specific topic.

In each task, a topic will be presented to you and you must write out a discussion on it within the time allowed. You must evaluate the topic, organize your ideas, and develop them into a cohesive and coherent response.

These tasks will not necessarily have a right or a wrong answer. You will be scored on how well you are able to utilize standard written English, organize and explain your thoughts, and support those thoughts with reasons and examples.

Tips for the Writing Section

For the writing section of this test, you will need to answer an integrated writing task, which involves a reading or speaking comprehension section with a writing response to the topic. The Independent writing task asks you to explain and support your own opinion about an issue.

TIP 1: INTEGRATED WRITING TASK

For the integrated writing task, you will need to understand and respond to written and **verbal input**. Try to take note of what is said so you can refer back to this information in your own responses for comparison or contrast.

TIP 2: INDEPENDENT WRITING TASK

For the independent writing task, you will need to write an essay explaining and supporting your own **opinion** regarding a subject. For this, you should try to be as organized as possible, making clear points and organizing them into meaningful paragraphs. Follow the introduction, body, and conclusion format if possible. Practice discussing common issues in this format and review your work to eliminate unnecessary information. Remember that extra information only slows down and can confuse readers.

TIP 3: GENERAL RECOMMENDATIONS

Try to learn **descriptive adverbs and adjectives** that can be used in many arguments rather than using common words. Descriptive language can keep readers engaged and provide more detail if used correctly. Practice using a **QWERTY keyboard**, which you will need to use during this test.

The Writing Process

BRAINSTORM

Spend the first few minutes brainstorming ideas. Write down any ideas you might have on the topic. The purpose is to extract from the recesses of your memory any **relevant information**. In this stage, anything goes down. Write down any idea, regardless of how good or bad it may initially seem. You can use either the scratch paper provided or the word processor to quickly jot down your thoughts and ideas. The word processor is highly recommended though, particularly if you are a fast typist.

STRENGTH THROUGH DIVERSITY

The best papers will contain **diversity** of examples and reasoning. As you brainstorm, consider different perspectives. Not only are there two sides to every topic, but there are also countless **perspectives** that can be considered. On any topic, different groups are impacted, with many reaching the same conclusion or position, but through vastly different paths. Try to "see" the topic through as many different eyes as you can. Look at it from every angle and vantage point. The more diverse the reasoning used, the more balanced the paper will become and the better the score will be.

Example:

The topic of free trade is not just two-sided. It impacts politicians, domestic (US) manufacturers, foreign manufacturers, the US economy, the world economy, strategic alliances, retailers, wholesalers, consumers, unions, workers, and the exchange not only of goods, but also of ideas, beliefs, and cultures. The more of these angles that you can use to approach the topic, the more solid your reasoning and the stronger your position.

Furthermore, don't just use information as to how the topic impacts other people. Draw liberally from your own **experience and observations**. Describe a personal experience that you have had and your own emotions from that moment. Anything you've seen in your community or observed in society can be expanded upon to further round out your position on the topic.

Once you have finished with your creative flow, stop and **review** it. Which idea allowed you to come up with the most supporting information? It's extremely important that you pick an angle that will allow you to have a thorough and comprehensive coverage of the topic. This is not about your personal convictions, but about writing a concise, rational discussion of an idea.

Every garden of ideas gets weeds in it. The ideas that you brainstormed are going to be random pieces of information of mixed value. Go through them methodically and pick out the ones that are the best. The best ideas are **strong points** that you can easily write a few sentences or a paragraph about.

Now that you know which ideas you are going to use and focus on, **organize** them. Put your writing points in a logical order. You have your main ideas that you will focus on, and must align them in a sequence that will flow in a smooth, sensible path from point to point, so that the reader will go smoothly from one idea to the next in a logical path. Readers must have a sense of continuity as they read your paper. You don't want a paper that rambles back and forth.

START YOUR ENGINES

You have a logical flow of main ideas with which to start writing. Begin **expanding** on the topics in the sequence that you have set for yourself. Pace yourself. Don't spend too much time on any one of the ideas that you are expanding on. You want to have time for all of them. Make sure you watch your time. If you have twenty minutes left to write out your ideas and you have ten ideas, then you can only use two minutes per idea. It can be a daunting task to cram a lot of information down in words in a short amount of time, but if you pace yourself, you can get through it all. If you find that you are falling behind, speed up. Move through each idea more quickly, spending less time to expand upon the idea in order to catch up.

Once you finish expanding on each idea, go back to your brainstorming session up above, where you wrote out your ideas. Go ahead and scratch through the ideas as you write about them. This will let you see what you need to write about next, and also allow you to pace yourself and see what you have left to cover.

Your first paragraph should have several easily identifiable features.

- First, it should have a quick **description** or paraphrasing of the topic. Use your own words to briefly explain what the topic is about.
- Second, you should explain your **opinion** of the topic and give an explanation of why you feel that way. What is your decision or conclusion on the topic?
- Third, you should list your "writing points." What are the **main ideas** that you came up with earlier? This is your opportunity to outline the rest of your paper. Write a sentence explaining each idea that will be explained in further depth in additional paragraphs. If someone were only to read this paragraph, he or she should be able to get a good summary of the entire paper.

Each of your successive paragraphs should expand on one of the points listed in the main paragraph. Use your personal experience and knowledge to support each of your points. Everything should be backed up by **examples**.

Once you have finished expanding upon each of your main points, wrap it up. **Summarize** what you have said in a conclusion paragraph. Explain your opinion of the topic once more and quickly review why you feel that way. At this stage, you have already backed up your statements, so there is no need to do that again. All you are doing is refreshing the reader's mind on your main points.

PUNCTUATION

If a section of text has an opening dash, parentheses, or comma at the beginning of a phrase, then you can be sure there should be a matching closing dash, parentheses, or comma at the end of the phrase. If items in a series are each separated by commas, then any additional items in that series will also need commas. Do not alternate punctuation. If a dash is at the beginning of a statement, then do not put a parenthesis at the ending of the statement.

WORD CONFUSION

"Which" should be used to refer to things only.

John's dog, which was called Max, is large and fierce.

"That" may be used to refer to either persons or things.

Is this the only book that Louis L'Amour wrote?

Is Louis L'Amour the author that [or who] wrote Western novels?

"Who" should be used to refer to persons only.

Mozart was the composer who [or that] wrote those operas.

PRONOUN USAGE

To determine the correct pronoun form in a compound subject, try each subject separately with the verb, adapting the form as necessary. Your ear will tell you which form is correct.

Example: *Bob and (I, me) will be going.*

Restate the sentence twice, using each subject individually. Bob will be going. I will be going. "Me will be going" does not make sense.

When a pronoun is immediately followed by a noun (as in "we boys"), say the sentence without the added noun. Your ear will tell you the correct pronoun form.

Example: *(We/Us) boys played football last year.*

Restate the sentence twice, without the noun. We played football last year. Us played football last year. Clearly "We played football last year" makes more sense.

Using Commas

FLOW

Commas break the flow of text. To test whether they are necessary, read the text to yourself and pause for a moment at each comma. If the pauses seem natural, then the commas are correct. If they are not, then the commas are not correct.

NONESSENTIAL CLAUSES AND PHRASES

A comma should be used to set off **nonessential** clauses and participial phrases from the rest of the sentence. To determine if a clause is **essential**, remove it from the sentence. If the removal of the clause would alter the meaning of the sentence, then it is essential. Otherwise, it is nonessential.

Example: *John Smith, who was a disciple of Andrew Collins, was a noted archeologist.*

In the example above, the sentence describes John Smith's fame in archeology. The fact that he was a disciple of Andrew Collins is not necessary to that meaning. Therefore, separating it from the rest of the sentence with commas is correct.

Do not use a comma if the clause or phrase is essential to the meaning of the sentence.

Example: *Anyone who appreciates obscure French poetry will enjoy reading the book.*

If the phrase "who appreciates obscure French poetry" is removed, the sentence indicates that anyone would enjoy reading the book, not just those with an appreciation for obscure French poetry. However, the sentence implies that the book's enjoyment may not be for everyone, so the phrase is essential.

Another, perhaps easier, way to determine if the clause is essential is to see if it has a comma at its beginning or end. Consistent, parallel punctuation must be used, and so if you can determine a comma exists at one side of the clause, then you can be certain that a comma should exist on the opposite side.

INDEPENDENT CLAUSES

Use a comma before the words *and, but, or, nor, for,* or *yet* when they join independent clauses. To determine if two clauses are independent, remove the word that joins them. If each clause can stand alone as a complete sentence, then they are independent and need a comma between them.

Example: *He ran down the street, and then he ran over the bridge.*

He ran down the street. Then he ran over the bridge. Both clauses are capable of being their own sentence. Therefore, a comma must be used along with the word "and" to join the two clauses together.

If one or more of the clauses would be a fragment if left alone, then it must be joined to another clause and a comma is not needed between them.

Example: *He ran down the street and over the bridge.*

He ran down the street. Over the bridge. "Over the bridge" is a sentence fragment and cannot stand alone. No comma is necessary to join it with "He ran down the street." Note that this does not cover the use of "and" when separating items in a series, such as "red, white, and blue." In these cases a

42

comma is not always necessary between the last two items in the series, but in general it is best to use one.

PARENTHETICAL EXPRESSIONS

Commas should separate parenthetical expressions such as the following: *after all*, *by the way*, *for example*, *in fact*, and *on the other hand*.

Example: *By the way, she is in my biology class.*

If the parenthetical expression is in the middle of the sentence, a comma is placed both before and after it.

Example: *She is, after all, in my biology class.*

However, these expressions are not always used parenthetically, so commas may not be necessary. To determine if an expression is parenthetical, see if you need to pause when you read the sentence. If you do, then it is parenthetical and needs commas.

Example: *You can tell by the way she plays the violin that she enjoys its music.*

No pause is necessary in reading that example sentence. Therefore, the phrase "by the way" does not need commas around it.

HYPHENS

Hyphenate a **compound adjective** that is directly before the noun it describes.

Example 1: *He was the best-known kid in the school.*

Example 2: *The shot came from that grass-covered hill.*

Example 3: *The well-drained fields were dry soon after the rain.*

USE YOUR EAR

Read each sentence carefully, inserting the answer choices in the blanks. Don't stop at the first answer choice if you think it is right, but read them all. What may seem like the best choice at first may not be after you have had time to read all of the choices. Allow your ear to determine what **sounds right**. Often one or two answer choices can be immediately ruled out because they don't sound logical or make sense.

CONTEXTUAL CLUES

It bears repeating that contextual clues offer a lot of help in determining the best answer. Key words in the sentence will allow you to determine exactly which answer choice is the best replacement text.

Example:

ARCHEOLOGY HAS SHOWN THAT SOME OF THE RUINS OF THE ANCIENT CITY OF BABYLON ARE APPROXIMATELY 500 YEARS _____ MESOPOTAMIAN PREDECESSORS.

1. as old as any supposed
2. as old as their supposed
3. older than their supposed
4. older than a supposed

43

In this example, the **key word** "supposed" is used. Archaeology would either confirm that the predecessors to Babylon were more ancient or disprove that supposition. Since supposed was used, it would imply that archaeology had disproved the accepted belief, making Babylon actually older, not as old as, so either answer choice C or D is correct.

Since choice D contains the word "a," this would be correct if "predecessors" was singular. Since "predecessors" is plural (with an "s" on the end), choice C must be correct.

Furthermore, because "500 years" is used, answer choices A and B can be ruled out. Years are used to show either absolute or relative age. If two objects are as old as each other, no years are necessary to describe that relationship, and it would be sufficient to say, "The ancient city of Babylon is approximately as old as their supposed Mesopotamian predecessors," without using the term "500 years."

SIMPLICITY IS BEST

Simplicity cannot be overstated. You should never choose a longer, more complicated, or wordier replacement if a simple one will do. When a point can be made with fewer words, choose that answer. However, do not sacrifice the flow of text for simplicity. If an answer is simple, but does not make sense, then it is not correct.

Beware of **added phrases** that don't add anything of meaning, such as "to be" or "as to them." Often these added phrases will occur just before a colon, which may indicate a list of items. However, the colon does not need a lengthy introduction.

The phrases "of which [...] are" in the below examples are wordy and unnecessary. They should be removed and the colon placed directly after the words "sport" and "following".

Example 1: *There are many advantages to running as a sport, of which the top advantages are:*

Example 2: *The school supplies necessary were the following, of which a few are:*

DON'T PANIC

Panicking will not put down any more words on paper. Therefore, it isn't helpful. When you first see the topic, if your mind goes blank, take a deep breath. Force yourself to mechanically go through the steps listed earlier.

Secondly, don't get clock fever. It's easy to be overwhelmed when you're looking at a page that is mostly blank, your mind is full of random, confused thoughts, and the clock is ticking down faster than you would like. But you brainstormed first so you don't have to keep coming up with ideas. If you're running out of time and you have a lot of ideas you haven't covered, don't be afraid to make some cuts. Start picking the best of the remaining ideas and expand on those few. Don't feel like you have to write down and expand all of your ideas.

CHECK YOUR WORK

It is more important to have a shorter paper that is well written and well organized than a longer paper that is poorly written and poorly organized. Don't keep writing about a subject just to add words and sentences, and certainly don't start repeating yourself. Expand on the ideas that you identified in the brainstorming session and make sure that you save a few minutes at the end to review.

Leave time at the end, at least a few minutes, to go back and **check over your work**. Reread and make sure that everything you've written makes sense and flows well. Clean up any spelling or grammar mistakes that you might have made.

As you proofread, make sure there aren't any sentence fragments or run-ons. Check for sentences that are too short or too long. If the sentence is too short, check to see if you have an identifiable subject and verb. If it is too long, break it up into two separate sentences. Watch out for any "big" words you may have used. It's good to use difficult vocabulary words, but only if you are positive that you are using them correctly. Your paper has to be correct, but it doesn't have to be fancy. You're not trying to impress anyone with your vocabulary, but with your ability to develop and express ideas.

Summary

Depending on your test-taking preferences and personality, the writing will probably be your hardest or your easiest section. You are required to go through the entire process of writing a paper in a brief amount of time, which can be quite a challenge.

Focus on each of the steps listed above. Go through the process of creative flow first, generating ideas and thoughts about the topic. Then organize those ideas into a smooth, logical flow. Pick out the best ideas from your list. Decide which main idea or angle of the topic you will discuss.

Create a recognizable structure in your paper, with an introductory paragraph explaining what you have decided on and what your main points will be. Use the body paragraphs to expand on those main points and have a conclusion that wraps up the issue or topic.

Save a few moments to go back and review what you have written. Clean up any minor mistakes and give it those last few critical touches that can make a huge difference. Finally, be proud and confident of what you have written!

Speaking

In the speaking section, a topic will be presented to you and you must provide a short speech in response to the topic. Both the preparation and the speech must take place within the time allowed. There is not a correct answer to the topic. You must evaluate the topic, organize your ideas, and develop them into a cohesive and coherent response.

There are three speaking assignments that you will have to perform. In the first task, you will be asked questions about your family life and in the second task, you will speak briefly about a specific topic with specific questions. The third task will require you to hold a conversation with the examiner regarding a specific subject.

You will be scored on how well you are able to utilize standard spoken English, organize and explain your thoughts, and speak clearly to address the question.

Of all the test sections on the IELTS, this is the easiest to prepare for. This is the test section that you can practice anywhere, in your car, in your room, on the phone, by yourself, or with someone else. After you successfully pass IELTS, you will be speaking English a lot, so you might as well prepare by speaking it at every opportunity beforehand.

Tips for the Speaking Section

The speaking section will require you to demonstrate your ability to speak English in both academic and informal settings. This involves speaking in an organized and clear manner without much preparation time. You will be asked to give six short speeches ranging from 45 to 60 seconds regarding a variety of topics.

TIP 1: ANSWERING THE QUESTION

The speaking section of the test provides you with very little time to accomplish your goal of answering a question. Make sure that you spend your time saying things that matter and avoid saying things that do not. To practice, record yourself speaking about familiar topics. Go back and listen to yourself and identify unnecessary information. Try answering again until you think you have answered the question without digressing.

TIP 2: SPEAKING CLEARLY

A major part of speech requires you to pace yourself and speak not too quickly or too slowly. Speakers should also place adequate emphasis on key words, such as important nouns and verbs in each sentence. For practice, record yourself speaking or have someone listen to you and point out areas that are confusing.

TIP 3: GRAMMATICAL ACCURACY

While speaking, grammatical accuracy plays a key point in clearly communicating what you mean. Try recording your responses to questions about familiar topics, and write down your answers or listen for grammatical errors. To help keep your grammar clear, make your points simple rather than complex.

TIP 4: ORGANIZATION

Similar to the way writing should be organized with an introduction, three main points, and a conclusion, short speeches should be organized to make sure that everything that is said is to the point or supports the main objective. Practice making short arguments with clear points.

TIP 5: USING TIME EFFECTIVELY

Remember that the speaking section provides you with only 15 seconds to prepare and 45 seconds to answer the questions. Practice timing yourself answering questions and take note if you are speaking too quickly or including unnecessary information. Try practicing with a variety of topics.

PRACTICE TIPS:

- Make and practice a list of familiar topics and a few that you may not know much about.
- Verbally practice retelling specific days (yesterday, a holiday, etc.). Make sure to practice using prepositions and other connecting words, such as first, next, then, throughout.
- Practice telling short stories from your experiences in under a minute.
- Read or listen to a story and retell it.

Record yourself and ask yourself the following questions:

- Did I complete the task?
- Did I speak clearly?
- Did I make any grammatical errors?
- Were my points organized?
- Did I use my time well?

Preparing to Speak

BRAINSTORM

Spend your preparation time thinking of your main answer and a few points supporting your conclusion, as if this were a written response. Time is key, so do not try to think of too many reasons, but only what can be explained simply and clearly.

THE CLEAR MESSAGE OF A SPEECH

When speaking, you should be focusing on three fundamental **factors**: ideas, organization, and support. The most important thing for you to consider is whether the main ideas are *logical and clearly expressed*. If the ideas are comprehensible, you should then consider whether they have been expressed in the *logical order*, or whether you have presented them in a disorganized fashion. Finally, you need to consider whether your main ideas have been adequately *supported* by logic or facts. Do you provide enough support for your arguments to remain credible? Is the evidence provided relevant to the main ideas?

EXHAUSTING THE POSSIBILITIES

You will be prompted with some basic questions. There are only so many possible basic questions that can be asked about someone, so you can easily be prepared for every possibility. Go through and write down all the possibilities and a good answer for each. When you're asked about your family, you don't have to struggle to come up with descriptions for your family members. Practice ahead of time and know what you're going to say. Right now, as you're reading this, stop and take a minute to answer each of the following questions. If these were asked in an interview, what would you say?

1. Please describe yourself.
2. Please describe your family.
3. Please describe your home.
4. Please describe some of your interests.
5. Please describe your job.
6. Please describe your studies.

This is important practice. Make sure that you can spend a minute or so answering each of these questions without having to take time to think of a good response. These are basic questions and you should have your basic answers ready.

TELL A STORY

Think about your favorite relatives. In many cases, they are your favorite because they are such raconteurs, or good storytellers. These are your aunts and uncles that can turn a simple trip to the grocery store into high adventure and keep you captivated and entertained. Even if you're not a natural storyteller, with a little thought and practice, even you can turn dull past experiences into exciting exploits.

Stories are your strongest weapon for demonstrating your mastery of speaking English. Some questions practically beg for stories to be told. These need to be compelling stories, real time drama, with you as the hero. Once you begin a quick, exciting story, you have set the tone.

The easiest way to prepare for these more difficult questions is to scour your memory for any exciting instance in your **past**, perhaps where you played a leadership role or accomplished a goal. This can be from any part of your past: during your education, at home with your family, doing a

48

project at work, or anything that you might have had a part in. Identify the main characteristics of the story so you have the details correct. Make sure you know the basics of what happened, who was involved, why it occurred, and how the events unfolded sequentially. You certainly don't want to stumble over the facts and repeat yourself during your response.

ONE SIZE FITS ALL

These basic stories are building blocks. Just as a piece of lumber can be cut into many different shapes and have many completely unique uses, each of your stories does not only answer one unique question. Your stories are **one size fits all**. With practice you will find that you can use the same story to answer two seemingly unrelated questions.

For example, a question about teamwork and a question about working under pressure can both be answered by a story about your experience playing intramural basketball. The story could describe how you had to work as a team in order to get into the playoffs, spending time practicing together, coordinating plays, and whatever was necessary for the team to advance. Alternatively, the story could focus on the shots that you made that season in order to win the game in the last few seconds of play under enormous pressure. The basic story is the same: your experiences playing basketball.

The questions were different, but you **customized** the story to fit the question. With practice you should be able to answer almost any question with just a few stock stories that can be customized.

FIND THE BRIDGES

Some questions will lend themselves more readily to a story than others. You must have a set of basic stories ready that can be modified to fit the occasion. You must "find the bridges" in the questions offered to make sure your stories get told.

In WWII, the US Army used Bailey bridges. Bailey bridges were made of prefabricated steel sections that were carried around and could be thrown together at a moment's notice, allowing the army to move quickly across any obstacle and get to their destination.

You need to find bridges, i.e. **opportunities to tell your stories**. Look for any chance to turn a standard question about anything, into a bridge to begin telling your story. For example, "What is your job title?"

On the surface that might not seem like the ideal bridge, but with a little insight your response might become:

"My job title is Product Line Manager. I am responsible for everything from the development of new products to the obsolescence of old products. Marketing, sales, engineering, and production of the entire product line fall under my responsibility. One of the products was even my own idea based on feedback I received from my interactions with our customers. In the first year, it alone had achieved a sales level of over..."

The key to remember is that just because a question is **closed-ended** (yes/no or one-word answers), you don't have to answer it as a closed-ended question. Answer the question asked, but then find a way to develop your answer into a bridge to a good story of yours. With an open mind, the most closed-ended of questions can become a launch pad into a story.

PRACTICE MAKES PERFECT

Don't try to answer every question spontaneously. You'll spend most of your time trying to think of what happened and repeating yourself. Beforehand, think of the classic stories you could tell and then **practice** going over them with your friends, explaining how you successfully achieved the goal or took charge and gave leadership to your group project. You don't want to have the story memorized, because it will become stale in the telling, but you want it to be smooth. This story must be live and in living color, so that a potential listener could see himself taking part and watching the situation unfold. Have your friends and family members quiz you by asking you random questions and see how well you can adapt to the question and give a clear response.

IELTS Practice Test

Academic or General Training?

The IELTS has two different versions: *Academic* and *General Training*. The two versions have the same requirements for the Listening and Speaking sections but different requirements for the Reading and Writing sections.

Before you begin taking your practice test, you may wish to verify which version of the IELTS you are required to take. Then, when you get to the Reading and Writing sections, you can either skip over the one that you are not taking or just take both for extra practice.

Good luck!

Mometrix

Listening

ADDITIONAL INSTRUCTIONS FOR THE TEST

There are four types of listening samples on the IELTS exam including conversations, monologues, academic conversations, and academic lectures or monologues. Each of the following may include fill-in-the-blank, multiple choice, or short answer types of questions. In the real exam, listening passages may only be listened to one time.

LISTENING PASSAGE 1: CONVERSATION

Listen to the audio and answer the following questions

> **Practice Audio: Listening Passage 1: Conversation**
> Visit mometrix.com/academy and enter code: 638610

Match the class with the speaker by writing the correct letter in the blank:

1. Claudia's class: _____

    a. Engineering
    b. Philosophy

2. Miguel's class: _____

    a. Engineering
    b. Philosophy

3. What was Claudia upset about?

    a. The status of a group project for her philosophy class
    b. A difficult project designing a bridge for her engineering class
    c. Her difficulty in understanding Aristotle's philosophies and influences
    d. Receiving a poor grade on her midterm exams

List the two components of the group project assignment on notable philosophers:

4. _____

5. _____

6. In Claudia's sentence: "Thanks for commiserating with me, Miguel," the word commiserating most nearly means which of the following?

    a. Communicating
    b. Correcting
    c. Agreeing
    d. Sympathizing

For questions 7-8, fill in the table below with the required information for Claudia's presentation:

Philosopher Information
Where and when he was born
Primary
7. _____ and
8. _____
Whom he influenced, and who influenced him

9. Claudia is stressed about the group project because it is worth _____ of her total grade.

10. Claudia said that she used to love _____, but now her opinion has shifted.

LISTENING PASSAGE 2: MONOLOGUE

For questions 11-13, label the correct rooms on the diagram below, using the letters from the box:

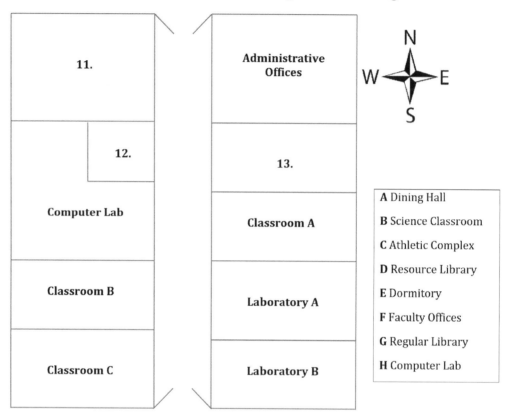

What two types of books can be found in the reference library?

14. _____

15. _____

In questions 16-17, match the name to the position by writing the correct letter in the blank:

16. Mia's faculty advisor: _____
   a. Dr. Helfric
   b. Dr. Lembas

17. Mia's chemistry teacher: _____
   a. Dr. Helfric
   b. Dr. Lembas

18. The computer lab wraps around the _____.

For questions 19-20, fill in the table below:

Administrative Offices
Here Mia can ask questions about:
Grades,
19. _____,
and her transcript

Computer Lab
Here Mia can:
Do online research,
Log in to her student account, and
20. _____

LISTENING PASSAGE 3: ACADEMIC CONVERSATION

Practice Audio: <u>Listening Passage 3: Academic Conversation</u>
Visit mometrix.com/academy and enter code: 126636

21. What is the main problem Connor is having?

a. He wants to become a chemistry tutor.
b. He cannot find time to make it to office hours.
c. He is struggling to understand the chemistry material.
d. He does not know where the Student Resource Center is.

22. Connor said that he tried looking at the textbook but found the material to be _____ and the examples to be _____.

What two days does the professor ask Connor to see her during office hours?

23. _____

24. _____

25. In the diagram below, which letter refers to the location of the student resource center? _____

Library, First Floor		Library, Second Floor	
Help Desk	Literature **A**	Reference Materials **D**	Group Study Area **E**
Study Rooms	History **C**		
B	Foreign Language **F**	Media Center **G**	

26. The two things Connor needs to bring to the Student Resource Center are his _____ and his _____.

27. What is meant by Connor's statement: "Availability wasn't the limiting factor; I think it was my pride."

a. I honestly felt proud about how I performed on the exam.
b. I honestly wasn't too busy; I think I just didn't want to admit that I needed help.
c. I honestly am not really busy but I wanted to make you proud.
d. There is a limit to how much time I can spend on this and still be proud of myself.

For questions 28-29, match the letter to the correct question:

28. The cost for a graduate student to use the Student Resource Center: _____

a. Free
b. A nominal fee

56

29. The cost for an undergraduate student to use the Student Resource Center: _____

    a. Free
    b. A nominal fee

30. Fill in the blank in the table below to show the different responsibilities of Connor and his professor to enable him to use the Student Resource Center:

Professor's Tasks	Connor's Tasks
Filling out a _____	Calling and going by the Student Resource Center to set up an appointment

LISTENING PASSAGE 4: UNIVERSITY LECTURE

> **Practice Audio: Listening Passage 4: University Lecture**
> Visit mometrix.com/academy and enter code: 945253

31. What does the professor argue is a strength of Shakespeare's plays and a quality that makes him a successful playwright in history?

    a. The fact that people have read his plays for centuries and his works are well-preserved
    b. That his works consider the complexities of human nature through character development
    c. The fact that he persuades audience members to be deviant
    d. The fact that his works teach readers about people and places from a vibrant period in history

32. What does the professor mean when she says, "I can see I'm losing some of you…"?

    a. Her students do not agree with her argument.
    b. Her students are dropping her course because it is too challenging.
    c. Her students are about to graduate.
    d. Her students are losing focus because they are worried about their exams.

33. The professor says that Shakespeare's main characters are written in general compliance with good and evil archetypes but their _____ are complex.

For questions 34-36, fill in the diagram below of Lady Macbeth's different roles. She shifted between these three roles:

The **34.** _____ role of a wife.

The **35.** _____ role of a leader.

The **36.** _____ behaviors of a seductress.

What two behaviors are necessary for Lady Macbeth to climb the social and financial ladder?

37. _____

38. _____

For questions 39-40, complete the summary below that lists the way Lady Macbeth alters herself to achieve her ambitions.

To seem more masculine, Lady Macbeth adjusts:
Her language and **39.** _____
To avoid suspicion, Lady Macbeth alters:
40. _____

Reading (Academic)

ADDITIONAL INSTRUCTIONS FOR THE TEST

In the academic reading portion of the exam, you will have to read material appropriate for someone who is seeking to enter college. You will have a variety of types of reading materials during your test and several types of questions. These materials can include passages, charts, and diagrams. Take your time and remember that all of the answers can be found in the source materials.

READING PASSAGE 1

Questions 1–14 are based on the following passage.

In 1603, Queen Elizabeth I of England died. She had never married and had no heir, so the throne passed to a distant relative: James Stuart, the son of Elizabeth's cousin and one-time rival for the throne, Mary, Queen of Scots. James was crowned King James I of England. At the time, he was also King James VI of Scotland, and the combination of roles would create a spirit of conflict that haunted the two nations for generations to come.

The conflict developed as a result of rising tensions among the people within the nations, as well as between them. Scholars in the 21st century are far too hasty in dismissing the role of religion in political disputes, but religion undoubtedly played a role in the problems that faced England and Scotland. By the time of James Stuart's succession to the English throne, the English people had firmly embraced the teachings of Protestant theology. Similarly, the Scottish Lowlands was decisively Protestant. In the Scottish Highlands, however, the clans retained their Catholic faith. James acknowledged the Church of England and sanctioned the largely Protestant translation of the Bible that still bears his name.

James's son King Charles I proved himself to be less committed to the Protestant Church of England. Charles married the Catholic Princess Henrietta Maria of France, and there were suspicions among the English and the Lowland Scots that Charles was quietly a Catholic. Charles's own political troubles extended beyond religion in this case, and he was beheaded in 1649. Eventually, his son King Charles II would be crowned, and this Charles is believed to have converted secretly to the Catholic Church. Charles II died without a legitimate heir, and his brother James ascended to the throne as King James II.

James was recognized to be a practicing Catholic, and his commitment to Catholicism would prove to be his downfall. James's wife Mary Beatrice lost a number of children during their infancy, and when she became pregnant again in 1687 the public became concerned. If James had a son, that son would undoubtedly be raised a Catholic, and the English people would not stand for this. Mary gave birth to a son, but the story quickly circulated that the royal child had died and the child named James's heir was a foundling smuggled in. James, his wife, and his infant son were forced to flee; and James's Protestant daughter Mary was crowned the queen.

In spite of a strong resemblance to the king, the young James was generally rejected among the English and the Lowland Scots, who referred to him as "the Pretender." But in the Highlands the Catholic princeling was welcomed. He inspired

59

a group known as *Jacobites*, to reflect the Latin version of his name. His own son Charles, known affectionately as Bonnie Prince Charlie, would eventually raise an army and attempt to recapture what he believed to be his throne. The movement was soundly defeated at the Battle of Culloden in 1746, and England and Scotland have remained Protestant ever since.

1. Which of the following sentences contains an opinion on the part of the author?

a. James was recognized to be a practicing Catholic, and his commitment to Catholicism would prove to be his downfall.
b. James' son King Charles I proved himself to be less committed to the Protestant Church of England.
c. The movement was soundly defeated at the Battle of Culloden in 1746, and England and Scotland have remained Protestant ever since.
d. Scholars in the 21st century are far too hasty in dismissing the role of religion in political disputes, but religion undoubtedly played a role in the problems that faced England and Scotland.

2. Which of the following is a logical conclusion based on the information that is provided within the passage?

a. Like Elizabeth I, Charles II never married and thus never had children.
b. The English people were relieved each time that James II's wife Mary lost another child, as this prevented the chance of a Catholic monarch.
c. Charles I's beheading had less to do with religion than with other political problems that England was facing.
d. Unlike his son and grandsons, King James I had no Catholic leanings and was a faithful follower of the Protestant Church of England.

3. Based on the information that is provided within the passage, which of the following can be inferred about King James II's son?

a. Considering his resemblance to King James II, the young James was very likely the legitimate child of the king and the queen.
b. Given the queen's previous inability to produce a healthy child, the English and the Lowland Scots were right in suspecting the legitimacy of the prince.
c. James "the Pretender" was not as popular among the Highland clans as his son Bonnie Prince Charlie.
d. James was unable to acquire the resources needed to build the army and plan the invasion that his son succeeded in doing.

4. Which of the following best describes the organization of the information in the passage?

a. Cause-effect
b. Chronological sequence
c. Problem-solution
d. Comparison-contrast

5. Which of the following best describes the author's intent in the passage?

a. To persuade
b. To entertain
c. To express feeling
d. To inform

6. What can be inferred from paragraph two about the author's view of 21st century scholars?

    a. 21st century scholars often disregard the role of religious views in historical political disputes.

    b. 21st century scholars make hasty observations about historical political disputes.

    c. 21st century scholars lack the details necessary to understand historical political disputes.

    d. 21st century scholars think that religion is never used in political disputes.

7. What is the nickname of the founder of a group called the *Jacobites*?

    a. Jacob

    b. The Deceiver

    c. The Pretender

    d. The Fool

8. Who does the passage say ascended the throne because someone else did not have a legitimate heir?

    a. King James Stuart

    b. Queen Elizabeth I

    c. King Charles II

    d. King James II

9. Which of the following best describes what the passage is about?

    a. The lineage of the current Queen of England

    b. The history of religions in Scotland and in England

    c. The role of religion in conflict between England and Scotland

    d. The history and origin of the Jacobites

10. Identify what belongs in the blank:

Queen Elizabeth I	James I	Charles I	Charles II	James II	?

    a. King Jacob I

    b. Bonnie Prince Charlie

    c. King James Stuart

    d. Princess Henrietta Maria

11. Based on the following sentence, what can you infer about the meaning of the italicized word? Mary gave birth to a son, but the story quickly circulated that the royal child had died and the child named James's heir was a *foundling* smuggled in.

    a. A prince

    b. An orphan

    c. A nephew

    d. An illegitimate child

12. What kind of tone does this passage have?

    a. Humorous

    b. Informative

    c. Solemn

    d. Sarcastic

13. Which piece of information is least important to the purpose of the passage?

a. Queen Elizabeth I died in 1603.
b. King James I had a Bible translation commissioned.
c. Bonnie Prince Charlie attempted to reclaim the throne.
d. King Charles II was believed to have secretly converted to Catholicism.

14. What was the end result of the conflict after the Battle of Culloden?

a. England and Scotland became Catholic as a result of the battle.
b. James the Pretender and his wife had to flee for safety.
c. This battle started conflict that would continue for generations.
d. England and Scotland have remained Protestant.

15. Which of the following would be the best title for this passage?

a. Bonnie Prince Charlie
b. Conflict between the Catholic and Lutheran Church
c. A History of England and Scotland
d. A History of the English Throne

READING PASSAGE 2

Questions 16–28 are based on the following passage.

Stories have been a part of the world since the beginning of recorded time. For millennia before the invention of the printing press, stories of the world were passed down throughout the generations through oral tradition. With the invention of the printing press, which made written material available to wide ranges of audiences, books were mass-produced and introduced into greater society. Before the printing press was invented, books had to be hand copied, which made them very difficult to make and very costly as a result.

For the last several centuries, books have been at the forefront of education and entertainment. With the invention of the Internet, reliance on books for information quickly changed. Soon, almost everything that anyone needed to know could be accessed through the Internet. Large printed volumes of encyclopedias became unnecessary as all of the information was easily available on the Internet.

Despite the progression of the Internet, printed media was still very popular in the forms of both fiction and nonfiction books. Similarly, newspapers are a format of reading material that have been widespread in availability and use. While waiting for an appointment, enduring a several-hour flight, or relaxing before sleep, books, magazines, and newspapers have been a reliable and convenient source of entertainment, and one that society has not been willing to give up.

With the progression and extreme convenience of technology, printed books will soon become a thing of the past. Inventions such as the iPad from Macintosh and the Kindle have made the need for any kind of printed media unnecessary. With a rechargeable battery, a large screen, and the ability to have several books saved on file, electronic options will soon take over and society will no longer see printed books.

Some people still cling to the old format of printed books as they enjoy owning and reading from paper materials. Although some people may say that the act of reading is not complete without turning a page, sliding a finger across the screen or pressing a button to read more on the next page is just as satisfying to the reader. The iPad and Kindle are devices

62

that have qualities similar to a computer and can be used for so much more than just reading. These devices are therefore better than books because they have multiple uses.

In a cultural society that is part of the world, and due to a longstanding tradition, stories will always be an important way to communicate ideas and provide information and entertainment. Centuries ago, stories could only be remembered and retold through speech. Printed media changed the way the world communicated and was connected, and now, as we move forward with technology, it is only a matter of time before we must say goodbye to the printed past and welcome the digital and electronic future.

16. What is the main argument of this essay?

   a. The iPad and Kindle are easier to read than books.
   b. The printing press was a great invention.
   c. The Internet is how people receive information.
   d. Technology will soon replace printed material.

17. What is the main purpose of paragraph 1?

   a. To explain oral tradition
   b. To explain the importance of the printing press
   c. To explain the progression of stories within society
   d. To introduce the essay

18. According to the essay, what was the first way that stories were communicated and passed down?

   a. Oral tradition
   b. Printed books
   c. Technology
   d. Hand writing

19. Which of the following statements is an opinion?

   a. Despite the progression of the Internet, printed media was still very popular in the forms of both fiction and nonfiction books.
   b. Although some people may say that the act of reading is not complete without turning a page, sliding a finger across the screen or pressing a button to read more on the next page is just as satisfying to the reader.
   c. With the invention of the Internet, reliance on books for information quickly changed.
   d. Stories have been a part of the world since the beginning of recorded time.

20. What is a secondary argument the author makes?

   a. Devices such as the iPad or Kindle are better than books because they have multiple uses.
   b. Books are still important to have while waiting for an appointment or taking a flight.
   c. Printed encyclopedias are still used and more convenient that using the Internet.
   d. With technology, there will soon be no need for stories.

21. What is the author's purpose in writing this essay?

   a. To inform the reader about the history of stories
   b. To persuade the reader about the merits of digital media
   c. To tell the reader an entertaining story
   d. To inform the reader about different types of print media

22. What kind of phrasing indicates the author's purpose?

a. The author states information in an unbiased way.
b. The author tells an entertaining story.
c. The author presents his information in a historical and factual manner.
d. The author asserts that one option is better than another.

23. What is the main reason the author gives for saying that books are going out of use?

a. Books are too costly to print.
b. Digital media is more convenient.
c. Storytellers prefer to keep an oral tradition alive.
d. People do not like to read as much.

24. Which of the following was not a reliable and convenient use that the author presents for books?

a. Relaxing before sleep
b. Waiting for an appointment
c. Studying for a test
d. Enduring a several-hour flight

25. Using examples from the passage, how does the author feel about the change in types of media for storytelling?

26. What would be a strong title for this passage?

a. Stories and How to Tell Them
b. Story-Telling and Technology
c. The Digital Future of Reading
d. A History of Print Media

27. The author gives several reasons that electronic devices are better than physical printing for modern story telling. Do you agree or disagree with the author? Provide examples from the passage.

28. Which best represents the organization of the information in the passage?

a. Problem-solution
b. Cause-effect
c. Chronological sequence
d. Comparison-contrast

29. According to the author, some people may say that the act of reading is:

a. Not complete without turning a page.
b. Not complete without the smell of a book.
c. Not complete without being able to highlight information.
d. Not complete without sliding a finger across the screen.

READING PASSAGE 3

Questions 29–42 are based on the following passage.

"So That Nobody Has To Go To School If They Don't Want To"

An Excerpt by Roger Sipher

A decline in standardized test scores is but the most recent indicator that American education is in trouble. One reason for the crisis is that present mandatory-attendance laws force many to attend school who have no wish to be there. Such children have little desire to learn and are so antagonistic to school that neither they nor more highly motivated students receive the quality education that is the birthright of every American. The solution to this problem is simple: Abolish compulsory-attendance laws and allow only those who are committed to getting an education to attend.

Most parents want a high school education for their children. Unfortunately, compulsory attendance hampers the ability of public-school officials to enforce legitimate educational and disciplinary policies and thereby make the education a good one. Private schools have no such problem. They can fail or dismiss students, knowing such students can attend public school. Without compulsory attendance, public schools would be freer to oust students whose academic or personal behavior undermines the educational mission of the institution.

Abolition of archaic attendance laws would produce enormous dividends:

- **First**, it would alert everyone that school is a serious place where one goes to learn. Schools are neither day-care centers nor indoor street corners. Young people who resist learning should stay away; indeed, an end to compulsory schooling would require them to stay away.
- **Second**, students opposed to learning would not be able to pollute the educational atmosphere for those who want to learn. Teachers could stop policing recalcitrant students and start educating.
- **Third**, grades would show what they are supposed to: how well a student is learning. Parents could again read report cards and know if their children were making progress.
- **Fourth**, public esteem for schools would increase. People would stop regarding them as way stations for adolescents and start thinking of them as institutions for educating America's youth.
- **Fifth**, elementary schools would change because students would find out early they had better learn something or risk flunking out later. Elementary teachers would no longer have to pass their failures on to junior high and high school.
- **Sixth**, the cost of enforcing compulsory education would be eliminated. Despite enforcement efforts, nearly 15 percent of the school-age children in our largest cities are almost permanently absent from school.

Communities could use these savings to support institutions to deal with young people not in school. If, in the long run, these institutions prove more costly, at least we would not confuse their mission with that of schools. Schools should be for education. At present, they are only tangentially so. They have attempted to serve an all-encompassing social function, trying to be all things to all people. In the process they have failed miserably at what they were originally formed to accomplish.

29. What is the main purpose for this passage?

    a. To report on students who do not want to go to school
    b. To discuss a variety of policies regarding school attendance
    c. To give reasons for the decline in standardized test scores in America
    d. To convince the reader that school attendance should not be mandatory

30. Based on the context of paragraph one, what could be a synonym for the word *compulsory*?

    a. Decisive
    b. Required
    c. Optional
    d. Frequent

31. What can you infer to be the author's view of modern educational policies?

    a. The author is indifferent to current policies.
    b. The author is satisfied with current policies.
    c. The author is against the current policies.
    d. The author is confused about the current policies.

32. Which of the following best sums up the passage?

    a. Standardized test scores are in decline and a change of policy would improve conditions.
    b. Schools do not teach and are currently used more as a social function instead of for education.
    c. Parents want an education for their children but are unable to get their children to behave.
    d. Communities need to save money to support better educational institutions.

33. Based on the context of paragraph three, what seems like the best synonym for the word *archaic*?

    a. Out-dated
    b. Vanishing
    c. Expensive
    d. Weak

34. Choose the sentence ending that would best fit the passage: Private schools don't encounter the same problems as public schools because…

    a. the students at private schools are better.
    b. private school teachers are higher quality.
    c. private schools are able to fail or dismiss students.
    d. private schools do not require their students to attend classes.

35. Which of the following is not a reason the author gives as a benefit for ending required attendance?

    a. Public esteem for schools would increase.
    b. Student transportation costs would decrease.
    c. Cost of enforcement would decrease.
    d. Grades would become more effective.

36. Based on the context in the final paragraph, what could be a synonym for the word *tangentially*?

    a. Expensively
    b. Confusingly
    c. Fully
    d. Slightly

37. Which of the following would be a strong concluding sentence?

    a. New attendance policies hold the power to improve test scores and make schools great again.
    b. With these changes, parents can ensure that the needs of their children are met.
    c. Parents should be responsible for ensuring that their children go to school, rather than the government.
    d. Through abolishing these outdated policies, schools can become all that they were meant to be.

38. How does the passage suggest that students who do not want to be at school undermine the mission of educational institutions?

    a. Schools are only interested in teaching those who want to learn.
    b. Students who do not want to come to class are more aggressive and bully others.
    c. Students who do not want to attend classes have harmful effects on other students.
    d. Schools strive to have the highest attendance rates possible and those who do not want to be in school do not always attend.

39. What does the author mean in using the word *birthright* to refer to American education?

    a. Americans are expected to be able to receive a quality education.
    b. Americans are literally entitled to education as an inheritance.
    c. By being born in America, one has a higher chance at becoming educated.
    d. Americans are expected to be educated as opposed to other nationalities.

40.

Benefits of Eliminating Mandatory School
Public esteem for schools would increase.
Elementary teachers would no longer have to pass their failures on to junior high and high school.
The cost of enforcing compulsory education would be eliminated.
?

Which of the following belongs in the table above?

    a. An end to compulsory schooling would require students who resist learning to stay away.
    b. There would be more and higher-paying jobs for teachers.
    c. Police officers would no longer have to babysit children.
    d. People would start thinking of schools as institutions for children.

41. How does the title relate to the passage?

a. The title directly relates to the passage, insinuating that school is not fun and should only be attended when a student wants to.

b. The title is satiric and mocks the notion that laws require students to attend school even if they do not want to.

c. The title is sarcastic and opposes the true meaning, that all students should go to school.

d. The title insinuates that students should be surveyed to find out which students actually want to attend school.

42. Using examples from the passage, how does the author suggest that attendance law reform would help with school performance?

Reading (General Training)

SECTION 1

Questions 1–6 are based on the following passage.

With today's busy society, fewer and fewer people are resting the recommended number of hours each night. Just a century ago, Americans slept an average of nine hours each night, and today the average has dropped to less than seven hours.

This is due to a variety of factors. Many careers are placing higher and higher demands on employees, requiring long hours with the promise of potential advancement. This and many other factors lead to increased stress levels, which makes sleep challenging even when someone has time for a full night's rest. One of the biggest changes to modern society is the advancement of technology: with news, entertainment, and communication available 24/7, it can be hard to shut down and rest. Finally, modern Americans face an abundance of health issues that were less common several decades ago. A culture of fast food, sedentary lifestyle, and no time for recreation and relaxation has wreaked havoc on the nation's health.

Outside of all these factors, each generation has its own reasons for losing sleep. Retired Americans struggle to adopt good sleep habits after years of staying up late and waking early to achieve the American dream. Middle-aged adults often feel pressure on all sides, trying to balance the tasks of taking care of aging parents and assisting grown children, as well as pursuing careers. Younger adults face the problem of succeeding in a challenging job market, as well as the urge to make their mark on the world, and are losing sleep as they try to figure out how to do so.

Each of these generations is increasingly relying on drugs and sleep technology to help them accomplish more and squeeze sleep into the few hours they allow. American consumers spend billions of dollars per year on specialty mattresses, phone apps for sleep, and sleep drugs. This doesn't even take into account the untold amount of money that sleep-starved Americans spend on coffee, energy drinks, and drugs for focus and attention to wake back up after a brief night.

Yet no amount of money can replace the much-needed time in bed for the mind and body to refresh. Just a few nights of good rest can begin to reduce stress, inflammation, and blood pressure. Risks for several diseases begin to lower. If people want to live happier and healthier lives, they must slow the pace, even if they don't seem to accomplish as much.

1. What is the main purpose of this passage?

    a. To show that each generation gets less sleep than the one before
    b. To describe the nationwide sleep problem in modern America
    c. To warn consumers of the dangers of sleep drugs
    d. To point out how technology has changed society

2. Which paragraph discusses the financial cost of America's sleep problems?

    a. Paragraph 1
    b. Paragraph 2
    c. Paragraph 3
    d. Paragraph 4

3. Americans were sleeping 9 hours per night in the early _____.
- a. 1800s
- b. 1900s
- c. 2000s
- d. none of the above

Do the following statements agree with the information given in the text?

In boxes 4–6 on your answer sheet, write:

TRUE if the statement agrees with the information

FALSE if the statement contradicts the information

NOT GIVEN if there is no information on this

4. The increasing prevalence of technology is single-handedly responsible for Americans' lack of sleep today.

5. Middle-aged adults have the hardest time getting enough sleep since they feel pressure from both the generation above and below them.

6. Consumer spending on sleep aids increases each year as more and more Americans struggle to sleep.

Questions 7–13 are based on the following pairs of passages.

Passage 1:

[A] Has technology changed the world for the better? Or is it actually detrimental to humanity and the world as a whole? There is no doubt that it is easier than ever to keep up with others around the globe, to be aware of world events, and to accomplish things that previous generations could only dream of. But is the cost of this accomplishment too high?

[B] Technology use has been linked to memory and attention problems in children as young as age two. Additionally, it contributes to the obesity epidemic as children sit in front of screens rather than playing outside. Children and technology just do not mix well.

[C] Perhaps even more alarming are the health hazards associated with technology. Vision problems can be caused by hours in front of a screen, and hearing loss is reported in conjunction with video games, music, and films. The constant radio waves, microwaves, and other output from technological devices bombard our bodies, endangering our health.

Passage 2:

[D] A century ago, moving across the nation or out of the country was an agonizing decision. For many of these people, they would never see the faces of loved ones again. Today, we can simply touch a few buttons on our phones and speak face-to-face with someone across the globe...or next door.

[E] Technology also gives us an unprecedented opportunity to teach our children. The Internet offers an unlimited supply of educational videos, games, and other resources. If a child is having trouble with reading or math, or even wants to learn to play the guitar, free resources are available 24/7.

[F] While many are concerned about the health dangers of a technological world, most of these claims are not valid. Certain types of radiation are dangerous, but safeguards are in place to protect consumers. All in all, technology is a far greater benefit than it is a risk.

For Questions 7–9, assess whether the following statements agree with the views/claims of the writer. Indicate "yes," "no," or "not given" in the boxes on your answer sheet.

7. The author of Passage 1 believes that technology may cause cancer in those who are constantly around electronic devices.

8. The author of Passage 2 believes that technology can enhance one's education.

9. The authors of Passages 1 and 2 agree that technology can be harmful for children.

For Questions 10–13, locate the specified information in the passages above and write the letters of the correct paragraphs in the boxes on your answer sheet.

10. Which paragraph contains the argument that playing music may cause hearing loss?

11. Where does one of the authors indicate that the health concerns may be less serious than some believe?

12. In which paragraph does the author with concerns about technology admit that it has provided new opportunities?

13. Which paragraph uses an emotional appeal to family bonds to make his or her argument in regard to technology?

71

SECTION 2

Questions 14–20 are based on the following passage and diagram.

Welcome to ABC Books! We look forward to having you on our team. You will be trained for various tasks and departments to give you experience in a variety of job duties, and so you can fill in for coworkers as needed. You will begin with general stocking and sales training, and move on to learn more in-depth customer service, inventory planning and scheduling, event planning, and other topics.

As you are on Schedule A, please arrive by 7:50 each morning so you can take care of any personal business before 8:00. In the break room there is a refrigerator where you can keep your lunch, and feel free to help yourself to the complimentary coffee (please keep it in the break room, though). When you've finished your personal business, clock in on the machine just outside the break room (the machine will accept clock-ins beginning at 7:55) and be on the sales floor by 8:00. We often begin the day with a brief staff meeting, so it is vital to be on time to hear any new assignments or policies that may be discussed at this time. The first hour is one of the most productive and crucial of the day, and it is important to be ready for business when the store opens at 9:00.

For your first several days, you will be shadowing different employees to become familiar with different departments. Before you leave each day, check with the assistant manager, Akisha, to see whom you will be working with the next day. For your first day you will be assisting Allison in the morning as she stocks shelves, and after lunch you will train with Lin at the cash registers. Depending on how quickly you master these skills, you may repeat the schedule several times or move on to other topics right away.

Lunch is from 12:00 to 12:45. You may bring your lunch and eat in the break room, or you may leave the store. There are many restaurants in the near vicinity, and you may bring food back to the break room to eat if you choose. Please be sure to clean up any mess and take home any leftovers rather than leaving them in the refrigerator overnight. Food left in the refrigerator past the end of your shift may be thrown away.

Schedule A shift ends at 4:45. Speak to a supervisor before clocking out to confirm that you have completed the day's assignments and to get any directions or advice for the following day. Do not clock out before 4:45 or the extra time will be deducted from your paycheck and may result in disciplinary action if it happens more than three times.

If you have any questions in the meantime, feel free to call or text one of your supervisors (see contact information on page 3 of your welcome packet). We look forward to working with you.

(A) Cash Registers		(B) Front Entrance	(C) Customer Service Desk
(D) Media Center	(E) Shelves		(F) Stock Room
(G) Clock-in Machine	(H) Break Room	(I) Utility Closet	

For Questions 14–17, fill in the schedule below, using no more than THREE WORDS from the text above.

7:50am	Arrive at work and take care of **14.** _____, then clock in
8:00am	Begin morning shift, assisting Allison with stocking shelves
9:00am	Store opens
12:00pm	Eat lunch in the **15.** _____ or leave to pick up lunch
16. _____	Begin afternoon shift, training with Lin at the **17.** _____
4:45pm	Clock out for the day

For Questions 18–20, fill in the blank with the correct letter from the diagram.

18. Go to Section _____ between 7:55 and 8:00, after taking care of personal business and before starting the official workday.

19. The morning shift will be spent in Section _____.

20. The afternoon shift will be spent in Section _____.

Questions 21–28 are based on the following passage.

At Workman's Academy, you will become proficient in the trade of your choice. This is an intensive, 18-month program that will lead to certification, marketable career skills, and assistance in obtaining a job. We have an outstanding track record of job placement, as well as career advancement, and our former students have a high rate of job satisfaction. It's time to get out of the rut of a futureless job and gain a skill that can change your life!

The first two weeks of the program will be devoted to an in-depth overview of the program and an introduction to each of the four main branches we offer. Refer to the descriptions of each of these branches below:

Department 1

Welding is our most popular career path at Workman's Academy. With a bright career future including high starting salary (entry level welders can earn as much as $20/hr) and a wide variety of career options, more and more students are seeking welding certificates. Benefits of our welding program include:

- Access to some of the nation's top instructors
- State-of-the-art machinery for practicing
- Thorough preparation for certification exams
- Assistance in job placement

Department 2

Another popular track is our electrician training program. This is a growing career field and an excellent time to begin the certification process. With training from Workman's Academy, you can build the electrician career of your dreams. Our training includes:

- Shadowing experienced electricians and training on real jobs
- Personalized training for certification
- Assistance in obtaining an internship

Department 3

Our plumbing career path comes highly recommended by many prestigious plumbing companies. We regularly receive requests from companies wishing to hire our graduates because of our program's excellent reputation. At Workman's Academy, you will receive the following benefits:

- Real-world training with local plumbers
- Exposure to a wide variety of commercial and domestic plumbing techniques
- Certification training (our students have a 92% passing rate)
- Assistance in career placement

Department 4

Our lineman program also has an outstanding reputation, and we frequently receive interview and hiring requests from companies across the state. You will be trained by field experts, who will not only give you invaluable knowledge and experience but will work with you personally to obtain your certificate. Benefits include:

- Equipment at discounted prices
- More hours of jobsite training than in the classroom
- Support in certification and job placement

For Questions 21–24, choose the correct heading for each of the paragraphs from the list below. Write the correct letter in the box to correspond with the number of the paragraph.

A	Benefits of Plumbing
B	Journey to a Lineman Career
C	How to Weld Anything
D	Jumpstart Your Electrician Career
E	License to Weld
F	What Does a Lineman Do?
G	A Life-Changing Experience at Workman's Academy
H	Pathway to Plumbing Certification

21. The best heading for Department 1 is:

22. The best heading for Department 2 is:

23. The best heading for Department 3 is:

24. The best heading for Department 4 is:

For Questions 25–28, match each statement with the correct department from the box below (answers may be used more than once):

A	Department 1 (Welder)
B	Department 2 (Electrician)
C	Department 3 (Plumber)
D	Department 4 (Lineman)

25. This department offers excellent equipment for students to use as they learn the trade.

26. In this department, students will learn how to do both commercial and domestic jobs.

27. This department offers a career path with a potentially high starting salary.

28. Students who choose this department will be able to obtain equipment at discounted prices.

SECTION 3

Questions 29–40 are based on the following passage.

Each fall, instinct sends multiple species of animals on a focused hunt for food. Some creatures such as squirrels gather food to hoard for the coming months of cold. Others consume large amounts of food, converting the extra calories to body fat, and then snooze the winter away while their bodies slowly utilize the fat to stay alive.

This phenomenon of hibernation is unique to endotherms, or warm-blooded animals. They are able to lower their body temperature, heart rate, breathing, and metabolism, thus needing far fewer nutrients for the winter months. Some animals lose over 25% of their body weight during hibernation but can wake months later without muscle atrophy. Some even give birth while hibernating.

Many animals are obligate hibernators. In other words, they enter hibernation on a regular schedule, so even if it's a mild winter and food is available, their bodies will still enter a period of torpor. This includes domesticated animals—even though a pet hedgehog may have a warm environment and abundant food, it will still automatically hibernate at a certain time of year. Obligate hibernators spend most of hibernation in the traditional sleep-like state, but periodically arouse, restoring heart rate and temperature to normal levels for brief times.

Other creatures may only hibernate if conditions demand. They are known as facultative hibernators and wait until cold weather or food scarcity make hibernation a necessity. They do not necessarily hibernate every winter, so if facultative hibernators are domesticated or the winter is unusually mild they may stay awake.

Ectotherms (cold-blooded animals) such as reptiles and fish do not technically hibernate, though many enter a similar state. They are unable to control their temperature and metabolism, and instead enter phases of what is known as dormancy, in which they can survive not only without food but also with very little oxygen. Thus certain kinds of turtles can bury themselves in mud and survive.

Why do only certain species hibernate? It is a defense mechanism for creatures that would have the most difficulty in cold weather. The animals that hibernate are the ones with high surface area to volume ratios. Their bodies struggle to adequately warm themselves in frigid weather so they hibernate to conserve energy. Animals that have lower surface area to volume ratios, or that can adapt to the weather by other means (such as humans building shelters and dressing warmly) do not need hibernation, however pleasant it may sound to dream the cold months away.

For Questions 29–32, choose the sentence ending that best fits, based on the passage above.

29. Animals do not need food in hibernation because they are able to _____.

    a. rouse periodically to search for food.
    b. stop the digestive process so their bodies do not use nutrients.
    c. slow body processes such as metabolism and breathing rate.
    d. use their extra fat and muscle tissue to sustain themselves.

77

30. Some animals hibernate only if _____.

    a. they need to because of cold weather and food scarcity.
    b. they are domesticated.
    c. they have a low surface area to volume ratio.
    d. they cannot enter dormancy.

31. Animals that experience dormancy need very little _____.

    a. food or warmth.
    b. water or oxygen.
    c. shelter or food.
    d. food or oxygen.

32. Instead of hibernating, some animals _____.

    a. adapt to their environment.
    b. eat excessive amounts of food before winter arrives.
    c. find a warm place to sleep.
    d. lower their metabolism so they don't need as much food.

For Questions 33–36, complete the sentences with words from the text, using no more than TWO WORDS.

33. Hibernation is only experienced by _____.

34. Animals that enter hibernation regardless of weather are known as _____.

35. Ectotherms may enter _____.

36. Hibernation occurs in animals with higher surface area to volume _____.

For Questions 37–40, provide a short answer from the text, using no more than THREE WORDS.

37. Endotherms, also known as _____, are the only creatures capable of hibernation.

38. Even _____ animals enter hibernation every year if they are obligate hibernators.

39. Animals that only hibernate when necessary due to weather are called _____.

40. Hibernation is a _____ to protect the animals that would have the most difficulty with the cold.

Writing (Academic)

ADDITIONAL INSTRUCTIONS FOR THE TEST

On the IELTS, you will be given two writing tasks to complete. The first task requires you to examine a chart or other source of data and provide a written explanation of the information. You must then write a response to a question asking about the main ideas and how the two sources of information relate. Your response should be at least 150 words.

The second writing task requires you to answer a question based upon your own personal views and experience. This may be asking if you agree or disagree with a statement and what reasons you have for thinking so. Responses for the independent writing task should be at least 250 words.

WRITING TASK 1

Use the chart and the lines below to answer the prompt in at least 150 words

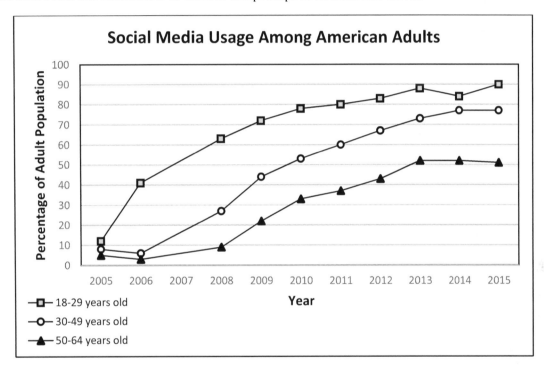

Describe the information presented in the chart. Make sure to describe the main features and any significant information that is presented.

WRITING TASK 2

Use the following passage to answer the prompt in at least 250 words.

Relationships and Social Media

The widespread phenomenon of mass communication through cell phones and the Internet has spurred enormous controversy. Many believe that people have become less able to build bonds with friends and family members as a result of technology. It is impossible to deny that social media is constantly changing the way that people interact with one another. With the advent of new technologies that allow for non-simultaneous and distant interaction, people all over the world are now able to build relationships in a way that was formerly not possible. Some might say that this is a negative trend, but this new development opens up unique and effective connections.

Do you agree or disagree with the writer's point of view? Please provide your reasoning for your answer.

Writing (General Training)

WRITING TASK 1

You should spend about 20 minutes on this task.

You have been working at Jim's Electronics, a retail establishment, for the past two years and feel that you deserve a raise. Write a letter to the manager requesting this raise. In the letter, you should:

- Describe your history at the store
- List the reasons you deserve a raise
- Describe your hopes for your future at Jim's Electronics and how you hope to improve your skills

Write at least 150 words. You do NOT need to write any addresses. Begin your letter as follows:

Dear Sir or Madam,

WRITING TASK 2

You should spend about 40 minutes on this task.

Social media is a powerful tool for not only communicating with friends but also spreading news and ideas. Unlike television, newspapers, and other traditional news media, social media allows instantaneous response and interaction. People from around the world can weigh in and share opinions. But this freedom also allows people to spread misinformation or to stir up unneeded controversy.

Do you believe that this is a valuable tool for news, and that the advantages of news-sharing on social media outweigh the disadvantages?

Give reasons for your answer and include any relevant examples from your own knowledge and experience.

Write at least 250 words.

Speaking

ADDITIONAL INSTRUCTIONS FOR THE TEST

When you take the real test, you will have a variety of tasks to complete for the speaking section. In **task 1**, you will answer several questions about familiar topics. These are short answer questions that should not take more than five minutes for the full task. These are common conversation types that you should practice in English as much as possible prior to your test.

Task 2 requires you to speak for up to two minutes about a specific topic. This topic is accompanied by reading a short passage including background information. Your response should include your views on the topic and include reasoning for why you believe so. You will have one minute to prepare and will have to provide a two-minute response in answering the question.

Task 3 includes a longer discussion between the examiner and the test-taker to discuss issues in more detail. Task three should not take more than five minutes.

SPEAKING TASK 1

ANSWER THE FOLLOWING SERIES OF QUESTIONS

FAVORITE PLACE
1. What is your name?
2. Where are you from?
3. Where was your favorite place to go when you were a child?
4. Was this place popular or private?
5. Why was this place so special to you?

SCHOOL SUBJECTS
1. What was your favorite subject in school?
2. Have you always been good at this subject?
3. What is the most useful thing about this subject?
4. How do you think this will affect your future?

SPEAKING TASK 2

Some people prefer classes that meet once a week in a single long session while others prefer courses that meet several days per week for a shorter duration. What is your opinion? Explain why.

    Preparation Time: 30 seconds
    Response Time: 1 Minute 30 seconds

SPEAKING TASK 3

HOLD A CONVERSATION WITH SOMEONE USING THE FOLLOWING QUESTIONS
- What are the typical reasons people choose their careers?
- How has this changed within the past few generations?
- Do you think this will continue to change in the future?

Answer Key and Explanations

Listening

1. B: Claudia is taking a **philosophy** class.

2. A: Miguel was taking an **engineering** class.

3. A: At the beginning of the conversation, listeners should recall that the female student, Claudia, informs the male student, Miguel, that she is stressed about a big project in her philosophy class. She says, "I love the material we are learning but I'm frustrated by a big assignment that's due next week." She later reveals to Miguel that it's a midterm group project. Miguel was the one who had the bridge project for engineering, so Choice B is incorrect. There is no mention of the fact that she is struggling to understand the philosophies; in fact, she says she's enjoying the material, so Choice C is wrong. She has not yet received the grade for the midterm because the project is due on Monday, so Choice D is incorrect.

4-5. Claudia says that they must write a **10-page paper** and give a **20-minute presentation** on notable philosophers.

6. D: *Commiserating* means to sympathize or feel pity for someone else. Miguel has been in a similar situation before – when he had to work on the bridge project with his engineering group but had to do most of the work himself – so he is able to relate to Claudia's situation and feels badly for her. He also says: "I don't envy the situation you're in." This means that he is glad he is not in her situation, because he knows it is not a good one to be in.

7-8. The project must include each philosopher's primary **ideas** and **interests**.

9. The group project is worth **40%** of Claudia's total grade.

10. Claudia states that she used to love **group projects**, but after this discouraging assignment her opinion has changed.

11. F: Tyler tells Mia that the **faculty offices** are across the hall from the administrative offices.

12. D: Tyler explains that the **resource library** is the small room with the computer lab wrapping around it.

13. A: Mia is told that the **dining hall** is on her left as she moves down the hall from the administrative offices.

14-15. The two types of books that Tyler mentioned could be found in the resource library are **encyclopedias** and a collection of **antique books**.

16. A: When Tyler points the faculty offices out to Mia, he tells her that she'll be coming back later to meet with her advisor. After the tour, he tells her that she will be meeting with Dr. Helfric to finalize her schedule, so we can infer that Dr. Helfric is her faculty advisor.

17. B: Tyler asks Mia if she is taking chemistry in the fall and mentions that Dr. Lembas is amazing. So we can infer that Dr. Lembas is the chemistry teacher.

84

18. When Tyler points out the **resource library**, he mentions that the computer lab wraps around it.

19. In the administrative offices, Mia can ask questions about her grades, **finances**, and transcript.

20. In the computer lab, Mia can do online research, log into her student account, and **print papers**.

21. C: The student is having trouble understanding the chemistry material, particularly balancing equations and different types of bonds. This is evident in the first several exchanges between Connor and his professor. Choice *A* is incorrect because he needs a chemistry tutor but does not want to become one. Choice *B* is wrong because he says he can make it to office hours and Choice *D* is true, in that Connor does not know where the Student Resource Center is, but this is not the main problem he was having. Instead, it is a secondary question that arises during the conversation about his difficulty with the chemistry material.

22. When Connor's professor asked if he had tried using the textbook to help him understand his chemistry problems, he answered that he had tried but found the material to be **dense** and the examples to be **confusing**.

23-24. Connor's professor asks him to come to her office twice a week after his trigonometry class on **Tuesday** and **Thursday**.

25. D: Connor's professor tells him that the Student Resource Center is on the second floor of the library, with the reference materials.

26. Connor is told to bring the **referral form** that his professor filled out and his **student ID** to the Student Resource Center.

27. B: "Availability wasn't the limiting factor; I think it was my pride" is best equated in the sentence: "I honestly wasn't too busy; I think I just didn't want to admit that I needed help." The limiting factor refers to what got in the way of accomplishing or doing something. Connor says availability (or time) was not the limiting factor, so he is not "too busy." When "pride gets in the way" it means that a person does not want to show or reveal that he or she doesn't understand something because that would be embarrassing and would negatively impact his or her self-esteem.

28. B: Connor's professor tells him that graduate students pay a nominal fee to use the Student Resource Center

29. A: The Student Resource Center is free for undergraduate students since it is included in their student fees.

30. Connor's professor told him that she would fill out a **referral form** that he could take to the Student Resource Center.

31. B: The professor argues that the strength of Shakespeare's plays and a quality that makes him a successful playwright in history is the fact that his works consider the complexities of human nature through character development. At the beginning of the lecture, she says: "As we've been discussing, one element of Shakespeare's writing that sets him apart from his predecessors, and arguably made him a great playwright, was his ability to create characters with intricate and interesting psychologies... These complexities um...evoke his audience's sympathies, and subsequently heightens their interest in the play." Choice *A* is a true statement, but it doesn't answer *why* he is considered a great playwright. While some of his characters are deviant (such as

Lady Macbeth), Shakespeare's plays don't necessarily *persuade* audience members to be deviant, so Choice *C* is incorrect. Choice *D* is not really mentioned in the lecture; while specific characters and kings are named, this is not emphasized as Shakespeare's lasting literary impact.

32. D: When the professor says, "I can see I'm losing some of you…" she is implying that her students are losing focus (she is losing their attention on her lecture). In this case, she believes it is because they are worried about their exam grades. She says: "I can see I'm losing some of you because I bet many of you have your minds on last week's midterm, so let's end our discussion here today and go over your test…" The other answer choices do not correctly translate this figure of speech.

33. The professor says that Shakespeare crafted his main characters with generally good or evil archetypes, but just like people in real life, these characters have complex **motives**.

34–36. The professor explains that Lady Macbeth shifts between the **passive** role of a wife, the **aggressive** role of a leader, and the **tempting** behaviors of a seductress.

37–38. The professor says that **self-effacement** and **politeness** are necessary behaviors for Lady Macbeth and her husband to climb the social and financial ladder.

39-40. The professor says that Lady Macbeth adjusts her language and **tone** to seem more masculine, while altering her **behavior** for the public eye to avoid suspicion.

Reading (Academic)

1. D: All other sentences in the passage offer some support or explanation. Only the sentence in answer choice D indicates an unsupported opinion on the part of the author.

2. C: The author actually says, "Charles's own political troubles extended beyond religion in this case, and he was beheaded in 1649." This would indicate that religion was less involved in this situation than in other situations. There is not enough information to infer that Charles II never married; the passage only notes that he had no legitimate children (in fact, he had more than ten illegitimate children by his mistresses.) And while the chance of a Catholic king frightened many in England, it is reaching beyond logical inference to assume that people were relieved when the royal children died. Finally, the author does not provide enough detail for the reader to assume that James I had *no* Catholic leanings. The author only says that James recognized the importance of committing to the Church of England.

3. A: The author notes, "In spite of a strong resemblance to the king, the young James was generally rejected among the English and the Lowland Scots, who referred to him as "the Pretender." This indicates that there *was* a resemblance, and this increases the likelihood that the child was, in fact, that of James and Mary Beatrice. Answer choice B is too much of an opinion statement that does not have enough support in the passage. The passage essentially refutes answer choice C by pointing out that James "the Pretender" was welcomed in the Highlands. And there is little in the passage to suggest that James was unable to raise an army and mount an attack.

4. B: The passage is arranged in a chronological sequence, with each king introduced in order of reign.

5. D: The passage is largely informative in focus, and the author provides extensive detail about this period in English and Scottish history. There is little in the passage to suggest persuasion, and the tone of the passage has no indication of a desire to entertain. Additionally, the passage is historical, so the author avoids expressing feelings and instead focuses on factual information (with the exception of the one opinion statement).

6. A: Paragraph two states that "Scholars in the 21st century are far too hasty in dismissing the role of religion in political disputes," which matches answer choice A.

7. C: The author states that the people of the Lowlands and England referred to young James as the Pretender, as he bore strong resemblance to the king, but did not hold true lineage to inherit the throne. Later, he would go to attempt to reclaim what he believed to be his rightful throne.

8. D: Paragraph three states that "Charles II died without a legitimate heir, and his brother James ascended to the throne as King James II."

9. C: This passage includes information about lineage, but generally seeks to inform and convince the reader that religion had a part in fueling conflict between nations, particularly England and Scotland.

10. B: Bonnie Prince Charlie was James II's heir. James Stuart was known as James I. James II was known as Jacob for the Latinization of his name, and Princess Henrietta Maria was married to Charles I, rather than being born into the family.

11. B: An orphan makes the most sense in this context and is discernable from the other answer choices. Neither a prince nor a nephew would need to be smuggled in. In addition, an illegitimate child was never referred to in this passage, which leaves orphan as the most fitting choice in this context.

12. B: Tone refers to the author's voice, or what kind of appeal he is making to the audience. In this passage, the author is attempting to inform the audience of a series of events in the history of English and Scottish royalty. The author is making an appeal, but makes his appeal with a tone that is informative sounding, as he grounds his argument in facts.

13. A: Whereas all of these answers are true, Queen Elizabeth's death is not necessary to the rest of the story. King James did commission a Protestant Bible translation, which could have been a major contributor to the conflict. Prince Charlie's and King Charles II's decisions also directly affected the conflict which this passage circulates around.

14. D: Whereas all of these answers are legitimate and came from the story, only one came as a result of this battle. The Battle of Culloden ended the confusion of religion between Scotland and England and they became completely Protestant nations.

15. D: A History of the English Throne is best suited for this passage since the passage explores the lives of multiple rulers of England. Answers A and C are not appropriate since the passage only mentions these two topics in passing. B is incorrect since the Lutheran church is never mentioned in this passage.

16. D: The main argument is stated in paragraph 4: "With the progression and extreme convenience of technology, printed books will soon become a thing of the past."

17. C: Paragraph 1 explains how stories have progressed, beginning with oral tradition and past the invention of the printing press. In context with the rest of the essay, this paragraph is important in explaining how stories progress and are provided within society.

18. A: In paragraph 1, it is stated that oral tradition was the main medium for storytelling before the invention of the printing press.

19. B: It is not a fact that "sliding a finger across the screen or pressing a button to read more on the next page is just as satisfying to the reader." Satisfaction is not something universal that can be proven for every reader. This statement is an opinion.

20. A: The author makes the argument in paragraph 5 that devices such as the iPad and Kindle are "therefore better than books because they have multiple uses."

21. B: The author's purpose in writing this essay is to persuade the reader about the merits of digital media. Although author uses history as part of the contextualization of his argument, and uses comparative information to help justify his points, this is more persuasive than informative due to his desire to convince the reader of the change from print to electronic books.

22. D: The author's purpose is evidently persuasive because of his use of captivating language when referring to digital media but not with print media. In addition, the author makes assertions that most people have already given up on print media and focuses on ways in which digital media is better. Print media is still very widely used, if not more used than digital books. The author uses some facts mixed in with opinions to make a convincing argument. If the author had used only facts and presented an unbiased argument, this passage could have been informative rather than argumentative. This passage was clearly not written for entertainment, as it does not seek to simply tell a story or use overtly descriptive language.

23. B: Each of these answer choices have merit, and are possibly true, but the only one given for the reason that books are going out of use is that digital media is more convenient. Books were costly when first made, but the passage gives no evidence of this at the moment. There is also no indication within the text provided that people do not like to read or that people still enjoy listening to stories.

24. C: In paragraph three, the author lists waiting for appointments, enduring flight durations, and relaxing before sleep as common uses for reading books. While studying for a test is a very effective use for books, the author does not list this as one of his points anywhere in the story.

25. Example Response: The author's purpose in writing this passage is to convince the reader that digital books are better than printed books. He even ends the passage with words such as "move forward" and an encouragement that "it is only a matter of time before we must say goodbye to the printed past and welcome the digital and electronic future." This language associates the past with print and the future with electronic, which indicates an excitement for the change, as opposed to resisting change.

26. C: Although this story begins by talking about storytelling, it centers more on the media format than on storytelling itself. It also acts more as a persuasive essay and not fully historical or informative. "The Digital Future of Reading" is more fitting than "A History of Print Media."

27. Example Response: The author gives a list of large screens, the ability to have several books saved on file, and the ability to recharge a device as reasons that digital media are as good as or better than printed media. These arguments are valid, in my opinion, because they save space, money, and can help the environment by reducing need for paper production. Printing books was useful for a time, but is no longer the logical choice in a modern world.

28. C: The passage is primarily organized in a chronological sequence to demonstrate progress into the future. At times the author does use comparisons, but looking at each paragraph, the author begins with the early forms of storytelling, continuing into print media, and finally into the modern electronic reading devices. The chronological sequencing contributes to his argument that electronic books are the way of the future.

29. A: The author uses a straw man argument to compare why people choose books versus digital reading devices. In paragraph five, the author gives the position that some people prefer printed books by saying that "reading is not complete without turning a page."

29. D: The main purpose of this passage is to convince the reader that school attendance should not be mandatory because it keeps students who want to learn from actually learning. The author does not go into the details of any attendance policies and only uses the decline in standardized test scores in America as an introduction to his actual topic. Whereas the other answers have pieces of information included in the passage, answer D is the only answer that sums up the main purpose of this passage.

30. B: The word *compulsory* is mentioned a few times throughout the passage and is used to mean required or mandatory. This is well indicated by the topic of attendance and using phrases such as "allow only those who are committed to attend." *Frequent* is the only other viable option but can be disqualified by the context.

31. C: The main ideas of this passage indicate a hope for change and even a proposition for doing away with the current policies. He poses himself as having a strong understanding of how the current policies work and advocates against them.

32. A: The author begins the passage by stating that standardized test scores are in decline and says that these test scores indicate that the education system is ineffective. The author proceeds to suggest changing laws to improve the system. Answer choices B and C refer to points that the author made throughout, but do not follow the whole of what this passage hopes to accomplish.

33. A: The context indicates that these laws are costly as a result of their applications, but do not fully support *expensive* as a viable answer. A better choice would be *outdated*. This particular context indicates that the laws are not functioning but are lingering. The word *vanishing* contradicts the author's intent for using this word.

34. C: This passage alludes to the fact that private schools have different regulations than public schools and are more easily able to fail or expel students. Whereas some of the other answer choices are potentially true, the only one that is indicated by paragraph two is answer C.

35. B: Each of the answers listed are given in paragraph three in the author's main list of benefits for a change of policy with exception to a decrease in the costs of transporting students.

36. D: For this context, the only meaning that could clearly apply is slightly or barely, as the author suggests that students are barely taught in schools with the conditions of the present education system.

37. D: Answer D is the best choice because it restates the author's position on the main issue and his plan to resolve the issue.

38. C: Answers A, B, and D were not indicated at all by the passage, although they may be true. Answer C was suggested in paragraph 1 – that the students who do not want to come to school are so antagonistic to learning that neither they nor the students who do want to come to school are able to learn effectively. The passage does not suggest any details as to how they might harm or distract other students.

39. A: The author uses the word *birthright* in a metaphorical sense to insinuate that all Americans should have the opportunity to receive a good education and that others should not be able to infringe on that right. Birthrights typically refer to familial property inheritances and not necessarily constitutionally or nationally given rights. Answers C and D are not insinuated at all with the passage.

40. A: In the list within the passages, it is said that an end to compulsory schooling would require students who resist learning to stay away. None of the other answers appear, even if they may be an implication of the author's point of view.

41. B: The title "So That Nobody Has To Go To School If They Don't Want To" is a more lighthearted sounding title than the serious excerpt that it describes. This could be mocking either those who do not want to attend school or the laws that require all children to go to school. Perhaps the author wrote the title in a lighthearted manner to attract readers rather than seeming overly harsh. Satire often makes use of over- or under-exaggeration, striking a humorous appeal to criticize a serious subject.

42. Example Response: The author provides several reasons why attendance law reform would help with school performance. By removing non-committed students from school, averages will easily go up. Furthermore, there will be fewer disciplinary issues causing distractions in the classroom. Teachers will be able to focus on teaching, and learning will, as a result, be much improved as a whole.

Reading (General Training)

1. B: The passage points out the problem of low sleep that affects large numbers of Americans. It mentions the differences in generations but does not state that each generation sleeps less than the previous one (A). It makes no mention of whether sleep drugs are dangerous (C) and the only mention of technology changing society is that it is a possible factor in today's lower sleep (D).

2. D: The fourth paragraph discusses American spending on sleep aids. None of the other paragraphs addresses this.

3. B: The passage states that Americans slept an average of 9 hours per night a century ago, or one hundred years. One hundred years ago was the early 1900s.

4. FALSE: The passage states that technology is only one of a variety of factors that contribute to the sleep problem.

5. NOT GIVEN: The passage does not indicate which generation has the hardest time getting enough sleep. It merely states the unique struggles of three different generations.

6. NOT GIVEN: Paragraph 4 states that Americans are "increasingly" relying on sleep aids, and that they are spending billions of dollars per year. But it does not state that spending increases each year.

7. NOT GIVEN: The author of Passage 1 mentions the "health hazards associated with technology," but does not make any mention of cancer.

8. YES: In Passage 2, Paragraph 5, the author lists several ways that technology can be used to enhance education.

9. NO: The author of Passage 1 indicates that technology is harmful for children, stating in the second paragraph that "children and technology just do not mix well," along with giving several reasons. The author of Passage 2, on the other hand, indicates that technology can be very helpful for children because of the educational opportunities.

10. C: The second sentence of Paragraph C states that "hearing loss is reported in conjunction with video games, **music**, and films."

11. F: In Paragraph F, the author suggests that some of the claims of health dangers are "not valid" and that "safeguards are in place to protect consumers."

12. A: The author of Passage 1 shares deep concerns regarding technology but acknowledges that "it is easier than ever to keep up with others around the globe, to be aware of world events, and to accomplish things that previous generations could only dream of."

13. D: The author of Passage 1 begins his or her argument by reflecting that moving away from family used to be very painful, but that technology has made this much less difficult. This author uses phrases like "agonizing decision" and "never see the faces of loved ones again" to make an emotional appeal to the reader.

14. Personal business/any personal business

15. Break room

16. 12:45pm

17. cash registers

18. G: The new employee is instructed to first take care of personal business, then clock in anytime after 7:55, and be on the sales floor by 8:00. So he/she should be in Section G (the clock-in machine) at some point between 7:55 and 8:00.

19. E: The passage states that the morning shift will be spent stocking shelves with Allison. Shelves are in Section E.

20. A: The passage states that the afternoon shift will be spent at the cash registers with Lin. Cash registers are in Section A.

21. E: Department 1 is welding, so look through the headings for one that applies to welding. Both Headings C and E refer to welding, but "How to Weld Anything" is vague and does not capture the main idea of obtaining a welding certification and job. "License to Weld" does a better job of referring to the main purpose of the academy.

22. D: The only heading that directly refers to learning the electrician trade is "Jumpstart Your Electrician Career," so it is the obvious choice.

23. H: Out of the two possible plumbing headings (A and H), only "Pathway to Plumbing Certification" refers directly to the purpose of the academy. "Benefits of Plumbing" is vague and could refer not only to a career but also to anyone in need of plumbing services.

24. B: Both choices B and F refer to linemen. "What Does a Lineman Do?" does not cover the main points of training and job placement, while "Journey to a Lineman Career" does encapsulate these main points.

25. A: The welding advertisement (Department 1) offers state-of-the-art equipment for students to practice on.

26. C: The paragraph for Department 3 (plumbing) mentions that students will learn both domestic and commercial techniques.

27. A: The section on Department 1 claims that welding jobs tend to have high starting salaries.

28. D: The Lineman advertisement (Department 4) offers students equipment at discounted prices.

29. C: Animals survive hibernation by slowing their body processes so that they do not use as many nutrients as usual. While they do rouse periodically (A), there is no mention of searching for food in the passage. The digestive process may slow, but the passage does not state that it completely stops (B). And while animals may use their extra accumulated fat, the passage states that they can emerge without muscle atrophy, so it is not logical that they use up muscle tissue during hibernation (D).

30. A: The passage states that facultative hibernators only hibernate if they need to because of cold weather or food scarcity. Animals that are NOT domesticated (B) are more likely to need hibernation. Animals with a LOW surface area to volume ratio (C) are less likely to hibernate. Since hibernation is unique to endotherms and dormancy is unique to ectotherms, it is illogical to say that an animal might enter hibernation if it cannot be dormant (D).

31. D: The paragraph on ectotherms states that these animals can survive with very little food or oxygen during dormancy. The other combinations are not mentioned.

32. A: The final paragraph states that some creatures adapt rather than hibernating. The other three choices are all actions that an animal takes before or during hibernation.

33. Endotherms: The second paragraph states that only endotherms experience hibernation.

34. Obligate hibernators: The third paragraph describes obligate hibernators, which enter hibernation regularly, regardless of weather conditions.

35. Dormancy: The fifth paragraph explains that while ectotherms cannot hibernate, they may experience dormancy.

36. Ratios: The sixth paragraph describes the animals that are likely to hibernate as the ones with higher surface area to volume ratios, since they have a more difficult time staying warm.

37. Warm-blooded animals: The second paragraph introduces endotherms and defines them as warm-blooded animals.

38. Domesticated: The third paragraph describes obligate hibernators, mentioning that even domesticated animals will enter hibernation.

39. Facultative hibernators: The fourth paragraph discusses facultative hibernators, which only hibernate if weather conditions make it necessary.

40. Defense mechanism: The sixth paragraph answers the question of why certain animals hibernate, stating that hibernation is a defense mechanism for those that would have the most difficulty with the cold weather.

Writing (Academic)

WRITING TASK 1

EXAMPLE RESPONSE

This is a line graph of social media usage in American adults from the year 2005 to the year 2015. It shows percentages of users for three age groups: 18-29, 30-49, and 50-64-year-old adults. In 2005, a very low percentage of around 10 used social media, and by 2015, more than 50 percent of all participants were using social media. The trend overall is that social media usage rose significantly and consistently for all groups over the course of the study. The graph is broken down further into age groups and shows that the youngest group, 18-29-year-olds were the fastest to adopt social media, with a major spike right from the start. Their usage leveled out to much smaller growth by 2010. The other two groups showed a slower trend at first, but by 2008, social media usage had steady growth from 30-49-year-olds and 50-64-year-olds. Throughout the graph, the younger participants always had the highest use rates, followed by the middle group, and lastly, the eldest group.

EXPLANATION OF EXAMPLE

In task 1, the test-taker needs to identify the study, which is done in the first sentence here. They then need to explain the overall data trends of the graph and reinforce the trends with data points. This example points out several trends and provided some explanation of how he or she found that answer.

WRITING TASK 2

EXAMPLE RESPONSE

Whereas technology such as cell phones has changed the way that people communicate, they have not weakened relationships at all. Mobile phones and social media are essential for communicating in both day-to-day life and in special circumstances.

Having a mobile phone has helped me in countless ways, such as making learning more efficient and less time consuming. As a result, I am free to use my extra time to do more things with my friends and family. Even when I am traveling or busy studying, I am able to keep in contact with people. In today's day and age, people are very busy and relationships can suffer from too little quality time spent. Texting and phone calls are no substitute for in-person communication, but they can certainly help to fill in the gaps when spending time in person is not possible.

The internet has helped me maintain my connections, even where mobile phones have failed. A couple of years ago, I was traveling in another country and was unable to see my family for two whole months. To make matters worse, I could not get a signal on my mobile phone to speak to my family. They must have been worried sick. Whenever I had a chance, I would find a place with an internet connection and would use social media to update my family as to what I was doing and remind them that I was safe. This kind of communication was essential to keeping my family from worrying about me while we were separated.

In my opinion, digital communication can never replace or weaken in-person connections but are a useful tool to help maintain relationships when needed.

EXPLANATION OF EXAMPLE

This answer is a good response because it addresses the question directly without wasting space. The response provides an outline in the second sentence of what arguing points the test taker is

94

going to make: that technology is useful for day-to-day and for special circumstances. The following two paragraphs provide examples that are relevant to the topic, and it is finally concluded with a repetition of the arguing point. Answers should be direct, provide clear examples, and everything that is written should relate directly to the topic.

Writing (General Training)

WRITING TASK 1

EXAMPLE RESPONSE

Dear Sir or Madam,

For the past two years, I have worked in your store. In that time, I have developed skills and learned to be the best employee I can. I now easily complete tasks that I could never have done as a new employee. After two years of service, I would like to respectfully ask for a raise.

There are several reasons I believe I deserve a raise. I have shown loyalty by working here for two years, while many of my coworkers have found new jobs after only a few months. I have been consistent to come in on my scheduled days, on time, and have only taken one sick day the entire time. Most importantly, I have a good work ethic and my skills are greatly improved. I have received many compliments on my customer service and good teamwork.

I believe that I can continue to develop my career at Jim's Electronics in the coming years. I am interested in learning more and training for new positions. Eventually I would like to work up to a position in management, where I can use my strengths of communication and organization.

Thank you for considering my request. I look forward to hearing from you.

Sincerely,

(Your Name)

EXPLANATION OF EXAMPLE

This response is over 150 words long, so it meets the length guidelines. Additionally, it clearly discusses the three bullet points from the prompt in logical order. The wording is clear and professional and the organization flows smoothly. The tone is polite and respectful but argues the main point without hesitation or apology.

WRITING TASK 2

EXAMPLE RESPONSE

Social media has doubtless changed the way that people interact and the way they receive information. There are many advantages: instantaneous access, an abundance of articles on any topic, and a wide variety of viewpoints. Consumers do not have to wait for the news to come on tv or for a paper to be printed. They can compare a multitude of articles or videos from varying viewpoints, and can weigh competing opinions.

However, social media is less reliable in many ways. "News" may be reported with little research, immensely biased standpoints, or even events that never happened. Articles can be written with no or very little truth, simply to stir up controversy or to falsely support a viewpoint. For a generation raised on social media rather than traditional news media, this presents a complicated gift: the world's events available with a click, but fact mixed with fiction.

So is social media news a valuable resource or a dangerous tool? Arguments can certainly be made for both sides, but a discerning consumer can gain a broader view by comparing the multitude of stances that are presented through social media and doing his or her own research with the abundant resources available online. The danger, of course, remains that many viewers will read an

96

article or watch a video and accept it as truth regardless of the misinformation it contains. And social media can certainly stir up controversy with emotional, unprofessional reporting. However, I have seen people enter heated arguments fully convinced of the "truth," only to enter into real discussion and sometimes even change their minds. My own mind has been broadened by chatting with people on all sides of an argument.

Further, it is important to remember that no report is entirely without bias. Every story on a tv news network and every article in a national newspaper is delivered from a particular view, even if the author tries to be impartial. It is better, overall, to see opposing viewpoints and make a discerning judgment for yourself, even if this requires more effort and exposes you to more misinformation.

EXPLANATION OF EXAMPLE

This essay meets the length requirements and backs up its points with multiple details, including personal experience. The essay considers both sides of the argument rather than just the "winning" side and acknowledges the value of the opposing side, as well as the weakness of the winning side. It then gives multiple reasons for choosing the winning side. Finally, it clearly states which side is chosen rather than just comparing and contrasting.

Speaking

SPEAKING TASK 1

FAVORITE PLACE SAMPLE RESPONSE

Examiner: First, I'd like you to introduce yourself and tell me about where you are from.

Test-Taker: Okay, my name is Benjamin, and I am from Hawaii. It's a group of islands with beautiful beaches and volcanic mountains. It's in the tropics and is part of the United States of America.

Examiner: So where was your favorite place to go in Hawaii?

Test-Taker: Kalihiwai, Kauai was my favorite place to go because my grandmother lived there.

Examiner: Was this place popular or private?

Test-Taker: There were very few people who lived there; under 100 people! Hawaii also has a lot of tourists and the bigger cities are usually loud and packed with people. It was always nice because my family was able to do whatever they wanted without running into crowds.

Examiner: Why was this place so special to you?

Test-Taker: It's a special place to me because my grandmother lived there. We would always go make campfires and look at the stars on the beach. We didn't see her often.

SCHOOL SUBJECTS SAMPLE RESPONSE

Examiner: What was your favorite subject in school?

Test-Taker: I always liked taking history classes.

Examiner: Have you always been good at this subject?

Test-Taker: No, I would fall behind sometimes because I couldn't remember the dates well! I didn't let that stop me from loving hearing about culture through the ages, though.

Examiner: What is the most useful thing about this subject?

Test-Taker: History reflects how people really are and that's important to know. The world is different, but the people are the same.

Examiner: How do you think this will affect your future?

Test-Taker: I think it's a good idea to learn from the past so that I can make better decisions for the future.

SPEAKING TASK 2

SAMPLE RESPONSE

I prefer when classes meet at least two to three times per week rather than just one long session. I find that it's hard for me to sit through a class that is more than an hour or so, and some courses offered by the university that only meet once a week are nearly four hours! I really struggle to maintain focus much longer than an hour and my hand gets tired from taking notes. Even if the

professor gives a break, it never fully rejuvenates me. The other issue I have with classes that only meet once a week is that it is hard to remember to keep up with the work. After you get through the marathon-session, you're so relieved to be done that it's easy to just dump the books in your room and before you know it, the week has rolled by and you haven't started on the work. When they meet every other day or so, you're forced to stay on top of the material better. Lastly, if you get sick and have to miss a class, if that's the one day the class meets, it's a big hassle to make up the work, and for that reason, some professors don't even allow absences without significantly penalizing your grade.

SPEAKING TASK 3

SAMPLE RESPONSE

Examiner: What are the typical reasons people choose their careers?

Candidate: I think it depends on the person. People can either choose based on money, or availability, but some choose to do something they are interested in.

Examiner: How has this changed within the past few generations?

Candidate: My parents and their friends all seemed to pick the jobs that paid well. They didn't expect their jobs to be fun, but just worked because it was what they were supposed to do. I think today, people are more willing to pursue jobs as artists or doing things that don't necessarily make much money. I'm not sure what is better, since there are benefits to both!

Examiner: Do you think this will continue to change in the future?

Candidate: I don't know, but I imagine there will be demand for some jobs and as my generation starts making families, some will change their minds and pursue jobs that make more money. I think with many people, the long-term choice will be to provide for their families rather than to do what seems fun.

Listening Transcripts

LISTENING PASSAGE 1: CONVERSATION TRANSCRIPT

Narrator: Listen to the following conversation between two students and then answer the following questions.

Male student: Hi Claudia, how's your philosophy class?

Female student: Oh, hey Miguel, it's pretty good. I love the material we are learning but I'm frustrated with a big assignment that's due next week.

Male student: Oh no. Why's that?

Female student: Well, it's a group project and we have to write a 10-page paper and prepare a 20-minute presentation about different notable philosophers, but my group doesn't seem to be taking the assignment seriously.

Male student: That sounds stressful. Does it count for a large percentage of your course grade?

Female student: Yes, that's the thing. This is our midterm project so it is worth 40% of our total grade. It's due on Monday and two of the people have yet to start their sections and the other student's piece was terrible.

Male student: Oh...what was wrong with it?

Female student: It really didn't satisfy any of the assignment requirements. His job was to cover Aristotle. Our professor gave us specific criteria to address for each philosopher, like where and when they were born, their primary ideas and interests, and who they influenced and who influenced them. Brian, the guy in my group, just focused on Ancient Greece in general and barely mentioned Aristotle, let alone his philosophical contributions!

Male students: That's awful. You know, that's the reason why I find group projects to be stressful. You never know who is going to be in your group and how motivated they are. Sometimes you end up having to do the nearly the whole project yourself or settle for a poor grade. Last year in my engineering class we had to design a suspension bridge using renewable resources in small groups. I had to carry the weight of the whole group since no one held up their end. It was so much work to do by myself.

Female student: Yeah...not fair. I might have to do that for this project. Before this, I always loved group projects, but now, my opinion has shifted.

Male student: Well Claudia, I wish you luck with the project. I don't envy the situation you're in.

Female student: Thanks for commiserating with me, Miguel. Have a nice afternoon.

LISTENING PASSAGE 2: MONOLOGUE

Hi, Mia; I'm Tyler. Welcome to Medfield Academy! This is my third year here and I know you're going to love it as much as I do. Let me show you around so you can get a feel for your new home.

We'll start right here at the north entrance of the main building with the administrative offices. You'll come here if you have questions about your grades, need to talk about finances, or want a

100

copy of your transcript. Across the hall are the faculty offices. You'll be meeting with your advisor here later today, after we finish the tour. Office hours vary from person to person, so be sure to see the schedules posted on their doors.

Now let's move down the hall. Okay, to your left, you'll find the dining hall. You'll be spending a lot of time here. Check the schedule in your welcome packet for freshman mealtimes. Across from the dining hall you'll find the reference library. It's that small room, with the computer lab wrapping around it. Our regular library is in the adjoining building to the west; we'll see it later. But you'll come to the reference library to use our extensive sets of encyclopedias or to research our antique book collection. In the computer lab you can do online research, log in to your student account to see assignments, or print papers.

Moving on, most of our classrooms are up that stairway, but the science classrooms and laboratories are here on the south end of the building. You'll have basic chemistry this fall, right? You'll be assigned a table in this lab. We have a lot of high-quality equipment, and Dr. Lembas is amazing. You'll learn so much.

Now let's walk outside and see the other buildings. Dorms are just east of here and the athletic complex is that building directly across the street. I'll show you where your room is and then bring you back to meet with Dr. Helfric to get your schedule finalized.

LISTENING PASSAGE 3: ACADEMIC CONVERSATION

Narrator: Listen to the following conversation between a student and his professor and then answer the questions.

Female professor: Hey Connor, thanks for staying after class. I won't keep you long, but I wanted to talk about your grades and progress in my course.

Male student: Yeah, I've been meaning to come to your office hours for some help. I guess I'm struggling to understand the chemistry material.

Female professor: Well, I'm glad you are trying to be pro-active about your studies and yes, you should always feel free to come to my office hours. If those times don't work for you, I am also happy to meet with you at an alternative time.

Male student: Thanks, but they are fine. I can come on Tuesdays and Thursdays after my trigonometry class. Availability wasn't the limiting factor; I think it was my pride.

Female professor: I appreciate your honesty and don't worry, a lot of students are nervous or shy to ask for help. But the good news is, you are here now we can start addressing your challenges. So, on the last exam, you got a 62. You got most of the questions about acids and bases correct, but it looks like you didn't get any of the chemical structure and bonding questions.

Male student: Yeah, balancing chemical equations went completely over my head and I don't understand the differences between ionic, covalent, and hydrogen bonds.

Female professor: Have you tried looking at this material in the course textbook?

Male student: I tried, but I found the writing to be very dense and the examples were confusing.

Female professor: OK. Don't worry. We have a lot of alternative resources that can help you. I'd like you to start coming to my office hours twice a week after your trigonometry class. Additionally, I think he would benefit from going to the Student Resource Center.

Male student: Hmm...what's that?

Female professor: It's a room in the library on the second floor with all of the reference materials. The University has a bunch of paid tutors who work with students in a variety of subjects. It's free for all undergraduate students because it is included in your tuition bill, and graduate students just pay a nominal fee.

Male student: Wow, that sounds great! I had no idea that we had a resource like that on campus. Do they have chemistry tutors?

Female professor: Yes. There are several great tutors to cover all of the sciences, including chemistry. I will fill out a referral form for you. All you need to do is call or stop by the Student Resource Center and set up an appointment. They will ask you for the referral form and your student ID.

Male student: Perfect. Thanks Professor Winter. I'll get right on this.

Female professor: That's great Connor. There is still plenty of time left in the semester to turn your grade around.

LISTENING PASSAGE 4: UNIVERSITY LECTURE

Narrator: Listen to the lecture in a literature class and then answer the questions.

Female professor: As we've been discussing, one element of Shakespeare's writing that sets him apart from his predecessors, and arguably made him a great playwright, was his ability to create characters with intricate and interesting psychologies. Many of Shakespeare's main characters are written in general compliance with "good" and "evil" archetypes, but just like generally "good" and "evil" people in real life, the motives of his characters are complex. These complexities um...evoke his audiences' sympathies, and subsequently heightens their interest in the play. Shakespeare's most famous characters are those that do not conform absolutely to typical protagonist and antagonist roles. These characters prevent audiences from considering and appreciating the play on strictly superficial levels.

So, now that we've had to chance to finish *Macbeth*, I think you'll see how Shakespeare's portrayal of Lady Macbeth contains these additional dimensions that make her character realistic and engaging. In public, she recognizes and behaves within her social limitations and expectations as a woman, but violates those boundaries while alone or with her husband. Lady Macbeth shifts between the passive role of a wife, the aggressive attitude of a leader, and the tempting behaviors of I don't know...a seductress, in order to advance her and her husband's social and financial status.

Lady Macbeth reveals her scheming and violent nature within her first few lines of the play. She is completely aware that she and her husband have common goals, but that without her influence, Macbeth himself lacks the primal instinct needed to commit the murder of King Duncan. Macbeth's horrible vision of murder is not his own, his ambition has been purposefully implanted by his wife. Macbeth's is extremely passive, and speaks in a tone much like that of a scared child; he asks his wife if they are going to be suspected of the murders. Essentially, the moment that Macbeth submits to his wife's leadership is the moment that the traditional marital and gender roles are reversed.

Do you guys see how the key to Lady Macbeth's strategy for gaining influence over her husband is to somewhat switch the gender roles within her marriage? Just before Macbeth arrives home, Lady Macbeth pleads "unsex me here." So, essentially, Lady Macbeth seeks to lose her female restrictions in order to gain total control over the situation, or…uh…what she sees as her opportunity to gain power over her husband. Lady Macbeth successfully "unsexes" herself by assuming the male role and aggressively taking matters into her own hands throughout the play. Lady Macbeth adjusts her language and tone to make herself more masculine in these instances, which intimidate Macbeth's actions in turn.

In order to avoid suspicion, Lady Macbeth alters her behavior for the public eye as well. She knows that self-effacement and politeness are necessary behaviors to adopt so that she and her husband are able to climb social and financial ladders. The tone of her speech as she addresses King Duncan is apologetic and submissive. She behaves this way to put the King at ease, and you know, probably to make him more susceptible to her husband's violence. Lady Macbeth plays both of these contrasting roles at the appropriate times in order to move the play in the direction which is most beneficial to her ambitions.

I can see I'm losing some of you because I bet many of you have your minds on last week's midterm, so let's end our discussion here today and go over your test, but next class, I want to pick up with the different styles of language Lady Macbeth uses to gain what she needs from the other characters in the play.

How to Overcome Test Anxiety

Just the thought of taking a test is enough to make most people a little nervous. A test is an important event that can have a long-term impact on your future, so it's important to take it seriously and it's natural to feel anxious about performing well. But just because anxiety is normal, that doesn't mean that it's helpful in test taking, or that you should simply accept it as part of your life. Anxiety can have a variety of effects. These effects can be mild, like making you feel slightly nervous, or severe, like blocking your ability to focus or remember even a simple detail.

If you experience test anxiety—whether severe or mild—it's important to know how to beat it. To discover this, first you need to understand what causes test anxiety.

Causes of Test Anxiety

While we often think of anxiety as an uncontrollable emotional state, it can actually be caused by simple, practical things. One of the most common causes of test anxiety is that a person does not feel adequately prepared for their test. This feeling can be the result of many different issues such as poor study habits or lack of organization, but the most common culprit is time management. Starting to study too late, failing to organize your study time to cover all of the material, or being distracted while you study will mean that you're not well prepared for the test. This may lead to cramming the night before, which will cause you to be physically and mentally exhausted for the test. Poor time management also contributes to feelings of stress, fear, and hopelessness as you realize you are not well prepared but don't know what to do about it.

Other times, test anxiety is not related to your preparation for the test but comes from unresolved fear. This may be a past failure on a test, or poor performance on tests in general. It may come from comparing yourself to others who seem to be performing better or from the stress of living up to expectations. Anxiety may be driven by fears of the future—how failure on this test would affect your educational and career goals. These fears are often completely irrational, but they can still negatively impact your test performance.

Review Video: <u>3 Reasons You Have Test Anxiety</u>
Visit mometrix.com/academy and enter code: 428468

Elements of Test Anxiety

As mentioned earlier, test anxiety is considered to be an emotional state, but it has physical and mental components as well. Sometimes you may not even realize that you are suffering from test anxiety until you notice the physical symptoms. These can include trembling hands, rapid heartbeat, sweating, nausea, and tense muscles. Extreme anxiety may lead to fainting or vomiting. Obviously, any of these symptoms can have a negative impact on testing. It is important to recognize them as soon as they begin to occur so that you can address the problem before it damages your performance.

Review Video: 3 Ways to Tell You Have Test Anxiety
Visit mometrix.com/academy and enter code: 927847

The mental components of test anxiety include trouble focusing and inability to remember learned information. During a test, your mind is on high alert, which can help you recall information and stay focused for an extended period of time. However, anxiety interferes with your mind's natural processes, causing you to blank out, even on the questions you know well. The strain of testing during anxiety makes it difficult to stay focused, especially on a test that may take several hours. Extreme anxiety can take a huge mental toll, making it difficult not only to recall test information but even to understand the test questions or pull your thoughts together.

Review Video: How Test Anxiety Affects Memory
Visit mometrix.com/academy and enter code: 609003

Effects of Test Anxiety

Test anxiety is like a disease—if left untreated, it will get progressively worse. Anxiety leads to poor performance, and this reinforces the feelings of fear and failure, which in turn lead to poor performances on subsequent tests. It can grow from a mild nervousness to a crippling condition. If allowed to progress, test anxiety can have a big impact on your schooling, and consequently on your future.

Test anxiety can spread to other parts of your life. Anxiety on tests can become anxiety in any stressful situation, and blanking on a test can turn into panicking in a job situation. But fortunately, you don't have to let anxiety rule your testing and determine your grades. There are a number of relatively simple steps you can take to move past anxiety and function normally on a test and in the rest of life.

Review Video: How Test Anxiety Impacts Your Grades
Visit mometrix.com/academy and enter code: 939819

Physical Steps for Beating Test Anxiety

While test anxiety is a serious problem, the good news is that it can be overcome. It doesn't have to control your ability to think and remember information. While it may take time, you can begin taking steps today to beat anxiety.

Just as your first hint that you may be struggling with anxiety comes from the physical symptoms, the first step to treating it is also physical. Rest is crucial for having a clear, strong mind. If you are tired, it is much easier to give in to anxiety. But if you establish good sleep habits, your body and mind will be ready to perform optimally, without the strain of exhaustion. Additionally, sleeping well helps you to retain information better, so you're more likely to recall the answers when you see the test questions.

Getting good sleep means more than going to bed on time. It's important to allow your brain time to relax. Take study breaks from time to time so it doesn't get overworked, and don't study right before bed. Take time to rest your mind before trying to rest your body, or you may find it difficult to fall asleep.

Review Video: The Importance of Sleep for Your Brain
Visit mometrix.com/academy and enter code: 319338

Along with sleep, other aspects of physical health are important in preparing for a test. Good nutrition is vital for good brain function. Sugary foods and drinks may give a burst of energy but this burst is followed by a crash, both physically and emotionally. Instead, fuel your body with protein and vitamin-rich foods.

Also, drink plenty of water. Dehydration can lead to headaches and exhaustion, especially if your brain is already under stress from the rigors of the test. Particularly if your test is a long one, drink water during the breaks. And if possible, take an energy-boosting snack to eat between sections.

Review Video: How Diet Can Affect your Mood
Visit mometrix.com/academy and enter code: 624317

Along with sleep and diet, a third important part of physical health is exercise. Maintaining a steady workout schedule is helpful, but even taking 5-minute study breaks to walk can help get your blood pumping faster and clear your head. Exercise also releases endorphins, which contribute to a positive feeling and can help combat test anxiety.

When you nurture your physical health, you are also contributing to your mental health. If your body is healthy, your mind is much more likely to be healthy as well. So take time to rest, nourish your body with healthy food and water, and get moving as much as possible. Taking these physical steps will make you stronger and more able to take the mental steps necessary to overcome test anxiety.

Review Video: How to Stay Healthy and Prevent Test Anxiety
Visit mometrix.com/academy and enter code: 877894

Mental Steps for Beating Test Anxiety

Working on the mental side of test anxiety can be more challenging, but as with the physical side, there are clear steps you can take to overcome it. As mentioned earlier, test anxiety often stems from lack of preparation, so the obvious solution is to prepare for the test. Effective studying may be the most important weapon you have for beating test anxiety, but you can and should employ several other mental tools to combat fear.

First, boost your confidence by reminding yourself of past success—tests or projects that you aced. If you're putting as much effort into preparing for this test as you did for those, there's no reason you should expect to fail here. Work hard to prepare; then trust your preparation.

Second, surround yourself with encouraging people. It can be helpful to find a study group, but be sure that the people you're around will encourage a positive attitude. If you spend time with others who are anxious or cynical, this will only contribute to your own anxiety. Look for others who are motivated to study hard from a desire to succeed, not from a fear of failure.

Third, reward yourself. A test is physically and mentally tiring, even without anxiety, and it can be helpful to have something to look forward to. Plan an activity following the test, regardless of the outcome, such as going to a movie or getting ice cream.

When you are taking the test, if you find yourself beginning to feel anxious, remind yourself that you know the material. Visualize successfully completing the test. Then take a few deep, relaxing breaths and return to it. Work through the questions carefully but with confidence, knowing that you are capable of succeeding.

Developing a healthy mental approach to test taking will also aid in other areas of life. Test anxiety affects more than just the actual test—it can be damaging to your mental health and even contribute to depression. It's important to beat test anxiety before it becomes a problem for more than testing.

Review Video: <u>Test Anxiety and Depression</u>
Visit mometrix.com/academy and enter code: 904704

Study Strategy

Being prepared for the test is necessary to combat anxiety, but what does being prepared look like? You may study for hours on end and still not feel prepared. What you need is a strategy for test prep. The next few pages outline our recommended steps to help you plan out and conquer the challenge of preparation.

STEP 1: SCOPE OUT THE TEST

Learn everything you can about the format (multiple choice, essay, etc.) and what will be on the test. Gather any study materials, course outlines, or sample exams that may be available. Not only will this help you to prepare, but knowing what to expect can help to alleviate test anxiety.

STEP 2: MAP OUT THE MATERIAL

Look through the textbook or study guide and make note of how many chapters or sections it has. Then divide these over the time you have. For example, if a book has 15 chapters and you have five days to study, you need to cover three chapters each day. Even better, if you have the time, leave an extra day at the end for overall review after you have gone through the material in depth.

If time is limited, you may need to prioritize the material. Look through it and make note of which sections you think you already have a good grasp on, and which need review. While you are studying, skim quickly through the familiar sections and take more time on the challenging parts. Write out your plan so you don't get lost as you go. Having a written plan also helps you feel more in control of the study, so anxiety is less likely to arise from feeling overwhelmed at the amount to cover. A sample plan may look like this:

- Day 1: Skim chapters 1–4, study chapter 5 (especially pages 31–33)
- Day 2: Study chapters 6–7, skim chapters 8–9
- Day 3: Skim chapter 10, study chapters 11–12 (especially pages 87–90)
- Day 4: Study chapters 13–15
- Day 5: Overall review (focus most on chapters 5, 6, and 12), take practice test

STEP 3: GATHER YOUR TOOLS

Decide what study method works best for you. Do you prefer to highlight in the book as you study and then go back over the highlighted portions? Or do you type out notes of the important information? Or is it helpful to make flashcards that you can carry with you? Assemble the pens, index cards, highlighters, post-it notes, and any other materials you may need so you won't be distracted by getting up to find things while you study.

If you're having a hard time retaining the information or organizing your notes, experiment with different methods. For example, try color-coding by subject with colored pens, highlighters, or post-it notes. If you learn better by hearing, try recording yourself reading your notes so you can listen while in the car, working out, or simply sitting at your desk. Ask a friend to quiz you from your flashcards, or try teaching someone the material to solidify it in your mind.

STEP 4: CREATE YOUR ENVIRONMENT

It's important to avoid distractions while you study. This includes both the obvious distractions like visitors and the subtle distractions like an uncomfortable chair (or a too-comfortable couch that makes you want to fall asleep). Set up the best study environment possible: good lighting and a comfortable work area. If background music helps you focus, you may want to turn it on, but otherwise keep the room quiet. If you are using a computer to take notes, be sure you don't have any other windows open, especially applications like social media, games, or anything else that could distract you. Silence your phone and turn off notifications. Be sure to keep water close by so you stay hydrated while you study (but avoid unhealthy drinks and snacks).

Also, take into account the best time of day to study. Are you freshest first thing in the morning? Try to set aside some time then to work through the material. Is your mind clearer in the afternoon or evening? Schedule your study session then. Another method is to study at the same time of day that you will take the test, so that your brain gets used to working on the material at that time and will be ready to focus at test time.

STEP 5: STUDY!

Once you have done all the study preparation, it's time to settle into the actual studying. Sit down, take a few moments to settle your mind so you can focus, and begin to follow your study plan. Don't give in to distractions or let yourself procrastinate. This is your time to prepare so you'll be ready to fearlessly approach the test. Make the most of the time and stay focused.

Of course, you don't want to burn out. If you study too long you may find that you're not retaining the information very well. Take regular study breaks. For example, taking five minutes out of every hour to walk briskly, breathing deeply and swinging your arms, can help your mind stay fresh.

As you get to the end of each chapter or section, it's a good idea to do a quick review. Remind yourself of what you learned and work on any difficult parts. When you feel that you've mastered the material, move on to the next part. At the end of your study session, briefly skim through your notes again.

But while review is helpful, cramming last minute is NOT. If at all possible, work ahead so that you won't need to fit all your study into the last day. Cramming overloads your brain with more information than it can process and retain, and your tired mind may struggle to recall even previously learned information when it is overwhelmed with last-minute study. Also, the urgent nature of cramming and the stress placed on your brain contribute to anxiety. You'll be more likely to go to the test feeling unprepared and having trouble thinking clearly.

So don't cram, and don't stay up late before the test, even just to review your notes at a leisurely pace. Your brain needs rest more than it needs to go over the information again. In fact, plan to finish your studies by noon or early afternoon the day before the test. Give your brain the rest of the day to relax or focus on other things, and get a good night's sleep. Then you will be fresh for the test and better able to recall what you've studied.

STEP 6: TAKE A PRACTICE TEST

Many courses offer sample tests, either online or in the study materials. This is an excellent resource to check whether you have mastered the material, as well as to prepare for the test format and environment.

Check the test format ahead of time: the number of questions, the type (multiple choice, free response, etc.), and the time limit. Then create a plan for working through them. For example, if you have 30 minutes to take a 60-question test, your limit is 30 seconds per question. Spend less time on the questions you know well so that you can take more time on the difficult ones.

If you have time to take several practice tests, take the first one open book, with no time limit. Work through the questions at your own pace and make sure you fully understand them. Gradually work up to taking a test under test conditions: sit at a desk with all study materials put away and set a timer. Pace yourself to make sure you finish the test with time to spare and go back to check your answers if you have time.

After each test, check your answers. On the questions you missed, be sure you understand why you missed them. Did you misread the question (tests can use tricky wording)? Did you forget the information? Or was it something you hadn't learned? Go back and study any shaky areas that the practice tests reveal.

Taking these tests not only helps with your grade, but also aids in combating test anxiety. If you're already used to the test conditions, you're less likely to worry about it, and working through tests until you're scoring well gives you a confidence boost. Go through the practice tests until you feel comfortable, and then you can go into the test knowing that you're ready for it.

Test Tips

On test day, you should be confident, knowing that you've prepared well and are ready to answer the questions. But aside from preparation, there are several test day strategies you can employ to maximize your performance.

First, as stated before, get a good night's sleep the night before the test (and for several nights before that, if possible). Go into the test with a fresh, alert mind rather than staying up late to study.

Try not to change too much about your normal routine on the day of the test. It's important to eat a nutritious breakfast, but if you normally don't eat breakfast at all, consider eating just a protein bar. If you're a coffee drinker, go ahead and have your normal coffee. Just make sure you time it so that the caffeine doesn't wear off right in the middle of your test. Avoid sugary beverages, and drink enough water to stay hydrated but not so much that you need a restroom break 10 minutes into the test. If your test isn't first thing in the morning, consider going for a walk or doing a light workout before the test to get your blood flowing.

Allow yourself enough time to get ready, and leave for the test with plenty of time to spare so you won't have the anxiety of scrambling to arrive in time. Another reason to be early is to select a good seat. It's helpful to sit away from doors and windows, which can be distracting. Find a good seat, get out your supplies, and settle your mind before the test begins.

When the test begins, start by going over the instructions carefully, even if you already know what to expect. Make sure you avoid any careless mistakes by following the directions.

Then begin working through the questions, pacing yourself as you've practiced. If you're not sure on an answer, don't spend too much time on it, and don't let it shake your confidence. Either skip it and come back later, or eliminate as many wrong answers as possible and guess among the remaining ones. Don't dwell on these questions as you continue—put them out of your mind and focus on what lies ahead.

Be sure to read all of the answer choices, even if you're sure the first one is the right answer. Sometimes you'll find a better one if you keep reading. But don't second-guess yourself if you do immediately know the answer. Your gut instinct is usually right. Don't let test anxiety rob you of the information you know.

If you have time at the end of the test (and if the test format allows), go back and review your answers. Be cautious about changing any, since your first instinct tends to be correct, but make sure

you didn't misread any of the questions or accidentally mark the wrong answer choice. Look over any you skipped and make an educated guess.

At the end, leave the test feeling confident. You've done your best, so don't waste time worrying about your performance or wishing you could change anything. Instead, celebrate the successful completion of this test. And finally, use this test to learn how to deal with anxiety even better next time.

> **Review Video: 5 Tips to Beat Test Anxiety**
> Visit mometrix.com/academy and enter code: 570656

Important Qualification

Not all anxiety is created equal. If your test anxiety is causing major issues in your life beyond the classroom or testing center, or if you are experiencing troubling physical symptoms related to your anxiety, it may be a sign of a serious physiological or psychological condition. If this sounds like your situation, we strongly encourage you to seek professional help.

Thank You

We at Mometrix would like to extend our heartfelt thanks to you, our friend and patron, for allowing us to play a part in your journey. It is a privilege to serve people from all walks of life who are unified in their commitment to building the best future they can for themselves.

The preparation you devote to these important testing milestones may be the most valuable educational opportunity you have for making a real difference in your life. We encourage you to put your heart into it—that feeling of succeeding, overcoming, and yes, conquering will be well worth the hours you've invested.

We want to hear your story, your struggles and your successes, and if you see any opportunities for us to improve our materials so we can help others even more effectively in the future, please share that with us as well. **The team at Mometrix would be absolutely thrilled to hear from you!** So please, send us an email (support@mometrix.com) and let's stay in touch.

> **If you'd like some additional help, check out these other resources we offer for your exam:**
> **https://mometrixflashcards.com/IELTS**

Additional Bonus Material

Due to our efforts to try to keep this book to a manageable length, we've created a link that will give you access to all of your additional bonus material.

Please visit https://www.mometrix.com/bonus948/ielts to access the information.

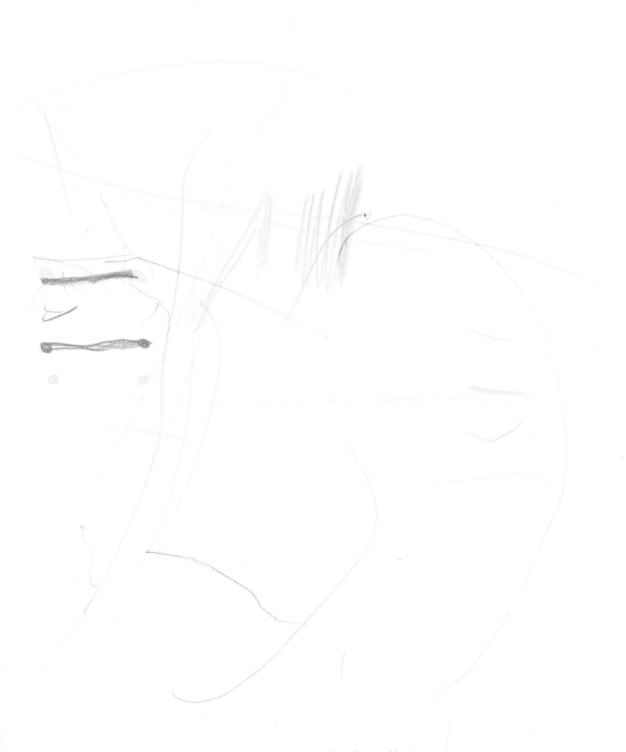

Manufactured by Amazon.ca
Bolton, ON